Welcome to Havana

Habana Vieja
© Jon Arnold Images/hemis.fr

Getting to Havana

BY AIR

José Martí International Airport

Code HAV - ☏ +53 7 2664644 - Located 15km southwest of the capital. All flights to Havana land here. There are three terminals; T3 handles international flights. In T3, there is an ATM on the upper level, a pharmacy, and a few eateries open 24/7.

TRANSPORT - CITY CENTER

Taxi

If you're staying in a *casa particular* (guesthouse) you can easily organize a taxi through your host. They'll charge you CUC25 (US$25) or CUC30. If you take a taxi from the airport taxi rank you'll pay CUC25. The ride to the city center is 30-40 minutes.

Car

A car is not essential for getting around Cuba, as the bus network is good and ride-shares easy to find. If you want to hire a car, book before the trip. In the provinces in particular, vehicles are scarce in high season and one can even speak of a shortage. You can pick up your hire car at the airport.

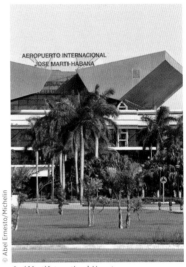

© Abel Ernesto/Michelin

José Martí International Airport

Bus

Although the bus network in Cuba is expansive, there is no bus service from the airport. The closest bus station is the Viazul station in Vedado. If you're going onward from Havana directly from the airport, you'll need to take a taxi to Vedado first (CUC25).

Classic car taxi
© S. Muylaert/Michelin

Unmissable

Our picks for must-see sites

Plaza Vieja★★★ 🕭 p. 26

Plaza de la Catedral★★★
🕭 p. 19

Farmacia y Droguería Taquechel★★★
🕭 p.24

Cementerio de Cristóbal Colón★ 🕭 p.48

Vintage car tour★★★
🕭 p. 7

4

The Malecón★★ ⊙ p. 42

Palacio de los Capitanes Generales★★★ ⊙ p. 14

Calle Mercaderes★★ ⊙ p. 24

Casa de la Obrapía★ ⊙ p. 25

Gran Teatro de La Habana★ ⊙ p. 34

Our top picks

💜 **See four centuries of architecture** in Habana Vieja (old town), a UNESCO World Heritage Site and center of the city's tourist attractions. Some of the handsome colonial buildings are in good condition; many, due to lack of resources and the prevailing humidity, are beautifully decrepit, but their 19th century facades and rich ironwork remain well worth a gander. *See p. 14.*

💜 **Follow in Hemingway's footsteps** by popping into the Ambos Mundos Hotel (he stayed in 511 and wrote *For Whom The Bell Tolls*), to El Floridita for a daiquiri, and then for a mojito at Bodeguita del Medio. If time allows, you can go out to his house Finca Vigía, now a museum 14km outside the city. *See p. 26.*

💜 **See an antique pharmacy** at Farmacia y Droguería Taquechel. It's a wonderfully historic space with magnificent wooden shelves, always filled with porcelain jars and glass bottles, among other ancient objects related to the pharmacy. This superb set looks timeless. *See p. 24.*

💜 **Stroll along the Malecón** at sunset, watching as the waves of the Gulf of Mexico crash against the seawall. The esplanade runs 8km, from the harbor in Habana Vieja up to Vedado. It's a pleasant walk and, when the sun sets, it's one of the hottest spots in Havana for hanging out with friends. *See p. 42.*

💜 **Party in an art factory** at Fabrica de Arte Cubano, a multi-level gallery/ tapas joint/live music venue/rooftop bar. It's open Thursday to Sunday only and is absolutely packed by 11pm with a fun mix of Cubans and visitors, all sipping mojitos. *See p. 70.*

© amlphoto/iStockphoto.com

Coco glace at Plaza Vieja

© Jon Arnold Images/hemis.fr

Ernest Hemingway's house - Finca Vigía

💙 **Cool off with coco glace**, a delightfully simple treat of coconut ice cream served in a coconut shell. You'll find a couple of vendors in Plaza Vieja. ✆*See p. 26.*

💙 **Use wifi in a park** at one of the green spaces dotted around Havana where a decent wifi signal is broadcast. Virtually no private residences have wifi, and though some hotels do, usually only guests can get on the network. At "wifi parks" do as the locals do and connect to one of the hotspots (you'll need to buy a scratch-off card good for one to five hours, usually being sold in the park). ✆*See p. 99.*

💙 **Cruise around in a vintage car**, one of the highlights of a trip to Havana. These gorgeous 1950s American classic cars are immaculately maintained. Drivers are very proud of their cars, and rightly so, which gleam and run like they're brand new. Pick them up around Hotel Inglaterra and go for a tour of the city with the wind in your hair. A perfect photo-op. ✆*See p. 34, p. 75.*

Havana and around in 3 days

DAY 1

▶ *Morning*

Most of the city's tourist sites are concentrated in **Habana Vieja★★★** *(p. 14)* Havana's Spanish colonial old town (a UNESCO World Heritage Site). Sumptuous mansions, handsome churches, large convents and lively squares fill a warren of streets crammed with apartments.

▶ *Afternoon*

After church-hopping (**Basilica Menor de San Francisco de Asis★★**; **Catedral de San Cristóbal★★★**; **Convento de Santa Clara★**) break for a modest seafood lunch at **La Taberna del Pescador** *(p. 68)*, where lobster, shrimp, octopus, and more are served to diners at just five tables. After lunch, continue getting lost in the colorful streets of Habana Vieja.

▶ *Evening*

A white-tablecloth dinner **Café del Oriente** *(p. 58)* is your destination tonight, a pianist plays a Classical repetoire as diners sip mojitos. Though seafood is prevalent here, fresh and delicious, there are good vegetarian options as well.

DAY 2

▶ *Morning*

Start in **Vedado★**, an upscale neighborhood with leafy avenues, mansions garlanded in bougainvillea, and music and cultural institutions. Its architectural elegance is exemplified in its museums and palaces of entertainment: the **Museo de Artes Decorativas★★**, **Museo Napoleónico★**, and **Casa de la Amistad**, all within reasonable walking distance of each other.

▶ *Afternoon*

Following a morning of walking Vedado's smart streets, take lunch at airy **Cafe Laurent** *(p. 73)*, on its large shaded terrace. The menu offers a choice of meats and seafood cooked to your liking. Vedado begins at **La Rampa★** (Calle 23), a wide thoroughfare edged with clubs, airline offices, and banks. At the sea end, the Art Deco **Hotel Nacional★** rises on a bluff; the nearby L-shaped **Edificio Focsa** offers one of Havana's best rooftop **views★★★**. The "palace" of ice cream, **Coppelia★**, and the palace of learning, **Universidad de La Habana**, are here. Some distances are too great to walk, so take a taxi.

8

9

Detail of the facade, Edificio Bacardí, Paseo del Prado, Habana Vieja

▶**Evening**

Walk along the Malecón and then a few blocks in to dinner at La Guarida *(p. 73)*. At first sight, this small Belle Epoque palace seems abandoned: by taking the superb marble staircase, you'll discover on the first floor the lounge (moldings, columns, decrepit paintings) open to the wind. To sup on: octopus carpaccio and pepper sauce; grilled chicken with honey and lemon.

DAY 3

▶**Morning**

Return to **Habana Vieja★★★** for what you haven't covered and for pleasant strolls past the beautifully crumbling buildings. Then take a taxi or *colectivo* (shared taxi) to Fusterlandia.

▶**Afternoon**

Fusterlandia is a magical mosaic world created by artist José Fuster. This beautiful public art installation spans several blocks, and Fuster plans to cover his entire neighborhood in bright mosaics. Pop into Fuster's studio, Taller-Estudio José Fuster, and you may see him at work. Free but donations recommended.

▶**Evening**

For your last dinner in Havana enjoy a warm sea breeze at **El Templete** *(p. 71)*, which specializes in fish (book ahead).

Discovering
Havana

Boys playing baseball, Plaza Vieja, Habana Vieja
© DANITA DELIMONT STOCK/Danita Delimont Agency/age fotostock

Havana today

Sitting just south of the Tropic of Cancer in the Atlantic Ocean, Havana occupies a northwest location on the largest of the Caribbean islands, Cuba. The city stretches westward and southward from a natural bay, accessed by a narrow inlet that protects the harbors therein. West of the bay, the Almendares River bisects the city from south to north. Cuba itself projects westward into the Gulf of Mexico, halfway between Florida (US) to the north and Mexico. This strategic location led the Spanish conquerors to call Cuba "the key to the Gulf." The country's—and Havana's—fate has long been tied to its geographic position.

The political, cultural and financial capital of Cuba, as well as a major port, Havana is a slowly modernizing metropolis of some 2.1 million ethnically diverse people. Though it is often portrayed as being stuck in time, the city is decidedly modern when compared to other Cuban cities. Luxury hotels here have many of the amenities expected of top international destinations. Wifi hotspots in hotels, public parks, and even the Malecón have been expanding rapidly in number. Tourism is on the rise and a number of cultural exchanges, commercial trade fairs and sporting events continue to attract international visitors, to the financial benefit of the city.

In the streets, **American-made automobiles** from the 1950s compete for pride of place with run-down

Havana's Neighborhoods

*Habana is divided into fifteen administrative districts called municipios. In this book, we cover the following neighborhoods: **Habana Vieja** (Old Havana) is the historic center of the city, and where most tourist sites are. To the west of Habana Vieja, **El Capitolio and the Prado** (Paseo José Marti) form what was the heart of the elegant city at the beginning of the 20C. Many tourists bypass **Centro Habana** and just follow the Malecón, the city's waterfront promenade, but to do so is to miss out on an authentic Habanero neighborhood, and home to the city's tiny Chinatown. Farther west, Centro Habana is succeeded by Plaza de la Revolución and then the upmarket neighborhood of **Vedado**. Here nearly all the streets are quiet, leafy, and lined in Belle Epoque villas, some crumbling but many lovingly restored. The neighborhood's main artery, the Rampa (north of 23rd Street), forms the modern and beating heart of the capital, and features many international hotels. Beyond the mouth of the Almendares river begins the municipio of Playa, which includes **Miramar**, a wealthier district where most embassies are located.*

© YinYang/iStockphoto.com

Malecón

Russian Ladas, yellow coco-taxis, bicitaxis, and an expanding fleet of modern vehicles. Everywhere you'll see *habaneros* lining up to squeeze aboard overloaded buses known as *guaguas*.

You won't find many ultramodern buildings in Havana, or a profusion of neon signs, ads or a shopping center on every corner. Indeed, there are practically no stores at all. There are no ads anywhere. Indeed it's Havana's antiquated charm holds great appeal for visitors (less so for Cubans). Despite years of economic sanctions and the resulting shortages, the people of Havana, the *habaneros,* have a ready smile. Music can be heard in nearly every nook of the city, and live salsa bands always draw crowds. On every street people are outdoors, talking to neighbors, kicking a ball around, fixing their cars, playing with their children. By night the capital emerges from the day's tropical languor and revs up to a nightlife charged with **Afro-Cuban rhythms**. At the bars and clubs of Havana you'll find happy, sweaty masses sipping mojitos and dancing until dawn.

Habana Vieja★★★

Facing Havana Bay, La Habana Vieja, or Old Havana, stretches east from Paseo de Martí (known locally as the Prado) to the harbor, and to the southwest beyond the central train station to La Regla district. Partly enclosed by a ring road that follows the footprint of ancient fortifications, Habana Vieja's historic heart holds the vast majority of the city's colonial buildings. A stroll through its narrow streets reveals a rich architectural heritage that earned this part of the capital UNESCO World Heritage status in 1982. Much restoration work is ongoing today. Despite reports of a few pickpockets, the area is quite safe and police are very present, but be smart at night on streets that are quite dark. Flat shoes are recommended or you're likely to trip on cobblestone.

▶**Access:** The whole of Habana Vieja is best explored on foot.
Area map: ***Maps II and III.*** Detachable map
▶**Tips:** If you have only a few hours in Habana Vieja, go directly to Calle Mercaderes, between Plaza de la Catedral and Plaza Vieja ***(Maps II and III)***.
🅸 **Infotur** – Calle *Obispo 524 between Bernaza and Villegas - ☏ 7-866-3333 - www.infotur.cu (Spanish only).*

14

PLAZA DE ARMAS ★★★

Map III-B2
Havana's oldest plaza (1582) was originally used for military parades and maneuvers, hence its name. It remained at the center of political life until the island gained formal independence in 1902, but it continued to play a significant role in Cuban politics well into the first half of the 20C. The plaza was enlarged to its present size in the second half of the 18C, landscaped and graced with fountains, benches and street lamps. Over time, it fell into decline but was entirely renovated in the mid-1930s. The centerpiece is a monument to **Carlos Manuel de Céspedes** (the "Founding Father" who initiated the wars of independence), carved by Sergio López Mesa in 1955.

Today, Plaza de Armas attracts hosts of people drawn by its bohemian atmosphere and languid vibe. Royal palms and *ceiba* (or kapok) trees shade the **central garden**, and sounds of traditional Cuban music waft over the square. Browse at one of the makeshift stalls that sell second-hand books, curiosities and Cuban memorabilia before settling in at a terrace cafe for some people-watching.

PALACIO DE LOS CAPITANES GENERALES★★★

Map III-B2
Filling the plaza's entire western side, this palace is a masterpiece of 18C Cuban Baroque architecture, designed by **Antonio Fernández de Trebejos y Zaldívar** (*see Palacio*

LA HABANA VIEJA
map II

CASTILLO DE LOS TRES REYES DEL MORRO

N

0   100   200   300 m

Castillo
de San Salvador
de la Punta

Monumento a los
Estudiantes
de Médicina

Parque Histórico
Militar Morro
Cabaña

Arcte de los Cocos

FORTALEZA DE
SAN CARLOS DE
LA CABAÑA

Museo de la
Comandancia
del Che Guevara

Bahía de la Habana

Canal de Entrada

see map III

Malecón

Túnel de la Habana

San Lázaro

Capdevilla

Genios

Refugio

Industria

Consulado

Trocadero

Colón

Morro

Zulueta

Ave. de los Estudiantes (Cárcel)

Ave. de las Misiones

Paseo de Marti (Prado)

Parque
de los Mártires

Máximo
Gómez

Capdevilla

Plaza
13 de
Marzo

Museo
Nacional
de la Música

Parque
Céspedes

Peña Pobre · Ave. Carlos M. Céspedes

PALACIO
PEDROSO

Cuarteles

Chacón

PLAZA
DE ARMAS

Museo de la
Revolución

Memorial
Granma

Hotel Sevilla

Museo Nacional
de Bellas Artes
(Arte cubano)

Teatro Lírico Nacional

Edificio
Bacardí

MANZANA
DE
GÓMEZ

Ave. Bélgica (Monserrate)

Animas

Virtudes

PARQUE
CENTRAL

Neptuno

TELÉGRAFO

Hotel
Inglaterra

Parque
Central

Gran
Teatro

El
Capitolio

Fábrica
Partagás

Parque
de la
Fraternidad
(Reina)

Industria

Paseo de Marti

Bélgica (Monserrate)

Bernaza

Cristo

Villegas

Aguacate

Compostela

Habana

Cuba

Aguiar

Empedrado

Progreso

O'Reilly

Obrapía

Lamparilla

Amargura

Brasil (Teniente Rey)

Muralla

Sol

Luz

Acosta

Jesús María

Merced

Paula

SANTO
ANGEL
CUSTODIO

PLAZUELA
DE SAN JUAN
DE DIOS

Calle

Obispo

Calle

Museo de
la Cerámica

Museo del
Chocolate

Casa de
las Hermanas
Cárdenas

Fototeca

Museo de la
Farmacia
Habanera

Casa del Conde de Jaruco

Santa Clara

Convento de
Santa Clara

Convento
de Belén

Arco
de Belén

Espíritu
Santo

Convento
de la Merced

Casa Natal
de José Martí

PALACIO
BALBOA

ESTACIÓN
CENTRAL

MURALLA

La Coubre

Ave de España

Fundación

Arsenal

Misión

Gloria

Apodaca

Cienfuegos

Economía

Corrales

Factoría

Suárez

Revillagigedo

Aguila

Florida

Misión

Esperanza

Máximo Gómez (Monte)

Dragones

Fuente
de la India

Asociación Cultura
Yoruba de Cuba

Egido

Agramonte

Picota

Compostela

Leonor

Pérez

Damas

Curazao

Inquisidor

Ignacio

Oficios

San

PLAZA
DE LA
CATEDRAL

Tacón

Mercaderes

San

San

BASILICA

Plaza
Vieja

Planetario

Hotel
Palacio
Viena

Oficios

Fuente

Lonja
del
Comercio

Plaza de
San Francisco

Aduana

Coche
Mambí

Fundación
Havana Club

REGLA

Oficios

Pedro

Clara

Bahía
de
la Habana

San Francisco
de Paula

FLORIDITA

Museo Nacional
de Bellas Artes
(Arte Universal)

SANTO CRISTO
DEL BUEN VIAJE

Ave. Lamparilla

PLAZA
DE ARMAS

17

del Segundo Cabo, p. 19) and Pedro Medina. The square, thick-walled building was erected on the site of Havana's first parish church (c. 1550), and took its present form in 1834, when major alterations were made. Home to the colony's Spanish governors until 1898, the strategic building was then used for a while by American governors during the post-independence occupation of Cuba by the US. In 1902 it officially became the presidential palace of the Cuban Republic, filling this function until 1920. The building was also the seat of Havana's municipal government for 176 years.

In 1968 the old palace was turned into the **Museo de la Ciudad**★★ *(open Tue–Sun 9:30am–4:30pm; 3CUC)*, a repository for paintings, documents, weapons, furniture and memorabilia that illustrate the major periods in Cuban history. Rooms open onto a lush **inner courtyard**★★ with a statue of Christopher Columbus in its center.

Palacio des los Capitanes Generales

On the ground floor, the island's oldest colonial vestige, a **cenotaph,** marks the death of a governor's daughter in 1557. A model of a sugar mill *(ingenio)* depicts the 19C process of making raw sugar from cane. On the upper floor, the former rooms of the governor's residence are appointed with exquisite furniture, delicate china and fine paintings. The very first Cuban flag is on view on this floor, as is Cuban painter Armando Menocal's (1863-1941) work *Antonio Maceo's Death*, depicting the last moments of the independence hero in 1896. The official end of Spanish rule was proclaimed in the Salon de los Espejos in 1899.

CASA DE LOS MARQUESES DE AGUAS CLARAS★★

Map III-A1
Located on the west side of the square, this elegant mansion (1775) now holds the popular **El Patio restaurant**. Its lovely inner **courtyard** has a fountain, and its balcony offers a sweeping **view** of the plaza. On the same side of the square is **Casa de Baños** (formerly the Public Baths), built in the 19C on the site of the cistern built in 1587. The ground floor has been turned into an art gallery. At the corner of the building is the **fountain** of Callejón del Chorro, which long ago first brought water

to the neighborhood. Situated at the end of the Callejón del Chorro is **Taller Experimental de Gráfica**, a leading graphic arts workshop selling contemporary works of art and offering instruction in the art of engraving *(p. 80)*. One of the most popular bar-restaurants in Havana, **La Bodeguita del Medio** *(see p. 59)* sits just west of the cathedral, on Calle Empedrado (between Cuba and San Ignacio).

CASTILLO DE LA REAL FUERZA ★★

Map III-B1
Corner of Calles O'Reilly and Baratillo - open every day but Mon 9am-5pm - 3 CUC.
Warlike cannons facing visitors, moats, thick walls: to the northeast of the Plaza de Armas, Havana's oldest fortress, built in 1558, remains mighty! The tower is topped by the city's emblem, the **Giraldilla**, a feminine weather vane completed in 1632 by sculptor Jerónimo Martínez Pínzon. The original of this effigy of **Doña Isabel de Bobadilla** can be found at the **Museo de la Ciudad** *(see p. 17)*. In the bowels of the *castillo* is a **museum** dedicated to the history of the fort and the discovery and exploration of the New World. Several ship models confirm that the port of Havana was a major center of shipbuilding between the 17th and 19th centuries. From the top of the tower, a beautiful view of Old Havana and the fortresses that completed the bay's defense system. *Return to the Plaza de Armas.*

Just to the left of the fortress, on the northern side of the square, the Marquis de la Torre had a post office *(Casa de Correos)* built in 1772, in perfect harmony with the neighboring **Palacio de los Capitanes Generales** *(p. 14)*. This building later hosted the Royal Stewardship of Finance, then army offices. In 1854, when it became the residence of the island's vice-captain general, it was named **Palacio del Segundo Cabo**★★ (palace of the Second in Chief). At the beginning of the 20C, it was the seat of the Senate, and in 1929 became the Supreme People's Court. It now houses a cultural institution.

Behind this palace, at 12 Calle Tacón, a pretty house from the early 18C hosts the **Cabinete de Arqueología** *(✆ 7-861-4469 - open Tues-Sun 9am-4pm, Sat 12:30pm - 1CUC)*, which has a very modest collection of pre-Columbian coins from Cuba, Mexico and Peru. *Turn left on Calle Empedrado to reach Plaza de la Catedral.*

PLAZA DE LA CATEDRAL ★★★

Map III-A1
Initially called Plaza de la Ciénaga (Swamp Square; it does sound more romantic in Spanish!), this 16C square was so named because it would become waterlogged in the rainy season. In 1587 a cistern was built on the square to supply fresh water to the local population and passing ships. Five years later, the neighborhood was connected to the **Zanja Real** (Royal Aqueduct) via the "royal channel" that ran through a

The best way to take in the view of Plaza de la Catedral and fully appreciate its layout is to get there early in the morning, before the hordes of tourists and musicians show up. If it storms overnight you'll be in luck; the rain washing clean the cobblestones leaves them wet and gleaming, and in the early morning light you can catch reflections of the plaza.

dead-end street known as Callejón del Chorro (Water Stream Alley) on the southwest side of the square. A true masterpiece of colonial design, the plaza was renamed in the 18C after its most prominent building. By then, the square had been drained, and this prime location, close to the harbor and the **Palacio de los Capitanes Generales** *(p. 14)*, attracted wealthy families who built handsome mansions around the plaza. Some of these have been converted to museums.

Catedral de San Cristóbal★★★
Open Mon–Fri 11am–2:30pm, Sat 10:30am–1pm, Sun 9:30am–12:30pm (Mass 10:30am). Access to bell tower 2CUC. The cathedral is best seen on a sunny day, when the edifice is bathed in golden light, enhancing its form and architectural details. Framed by asymmetrical towers, the Cuban Baroque **façade★★** is carved of fossil-embedded stone.
The original church was erected by Jesuits in 1727. After the king of Spain expelled the Jesuit Order from Cuba, the enlargement of the church was completed by Franciscans in 1777; in 1788 the church was upgraded to cathedral status. Its name honors **Christopher Columbus,** whose remains were reputedly brought from Santo Domingo and kept in the cathedral until removed to Spain upon Cuba's independence.
The **interior,** restored in the Neoclassical style, has a central nave and two aisles opening onto chapels. Above the **high altar★**, made of Carrara marble, are **frescos** by Italian painter Giuseppe Perovani. The mahogany **retable** features martyrs and apostles. Those who won't have the opportunity to visit the city of Santiago de Cuba can see a copy of the famous **Virgen de la Caridad del Cobre** (Cuba's patron saint) in the cathedral.

EL TEMPLETE

Map III-B1
This tiny Doric-columned temple *(Tues–Sat 9am–5pm, Sun 9am–12:30pm – 1 CUC)* was the first Neoclassical-style construction in Havana. It was erected in 1827 on the site where the **first Mass** was celebrated, back in 1519. In 1753 a hurricane uprooted the **ceiba tree** *(see box p. 29)* under which this memorable event took place and where the founding of Havana is commemorated each year on November 16. The following year, Governor F. Cajigal de la Vega had a column raised to mark the spot. The November 16 celebration is still held

© S. Muylaert/Michelin

LA HABANA VIEJA
Historic Center
map III

WHERE TO STAY		NIGHTLIFE	
Ambos Mundos (Hotel) **23**	Café O'Reilly **13**	Maragato **3**	
Florida (Hotel) **24**	Dominica (La) **14**	SHOPPING	
Marivelas (Casa) **25**	Doña Eutimia **15**	Taller Experimental	
Santa Isabel (Hotel) **26**	Esta No Es Un Café **16**	de Gráfica **9**	
	Mama Inés **17**		
WHERE TO EAT	Moneda Cubana (La) **18**	WHERE TO DRINK	
Bodeguita del Medio (La) **12**	Templete (El) **19**	Bodeguita del Medio (La) **4**	

in the garden today, under another stately ceiba tree. Inside the temple, notice the tryptich by **Jean-Baptiste Vermay** (1786-1833) depicting the first Mass, the first city council and El Templete's inauguration.

PALACIO DE LOS CONDES DE CASA BAYONA★★

Map III-A2
This palace facing the cathedral remains the oldest residence in the square. It's also named after its owner, Luis Chacón, who ordered its construction in 1720. The building was

successively the seat of the College of Clerks of Havana at the end of the 19C, a daily newspaper of the Republic, and then a nationalized rum company.

The structure, with a wonderful patio filled with exotic species, today houses the **Museo de Arte Colonial★★** (*☎ 7-862-6440 - 9:30am-6:30pm - 2CUC*). It's worth a visit for its rich collection of furniture, most of it made of mahogany. The complex, which comprises both civil and religious buildings, offers a complete panorama of the colonial period from the 17th to the 19th centuries. The museum also contains various architectural elements, including wrought iron gates, wooden balustrades and knockers, to which the old town owes much of its character. Also on display are some *mediopuntos*, pieces of colored glass or wood placed above the windows to filter the light. The windows of the building themselves are of beautiful stained glass. Also noteworthy is the very pretty set of *mamparas*, the interior doors typical of bourgeois residences.

PALACIO DEL MARQUÉS DE ARCOS★

Map III-A1
Admire the wrought iron balconies and columns that adorn the beautiful Baroque facade of this residence, built in the southeast corner of the square in 1741. Headquarters of the Royal Treasury from 1796, it became the central post office in the first half of the 19C, then the artistic and literary high school of Havana. You can find, drilled in the wall, an old **mailbox** identical to the one on Calle Obispo, near the **Plaza de Armas** (*p. 14*).

CASA DEL CONDE DE LOMBILLO★

Map III-A1
Every day but Sun 9am-4:30pm (Sat 1pm) - free.
Just to the right of the cathedral is this house, built in the first half of the 18C for the Pedroso and Florencia family, whose descendants received the title of count in 1871. Now the headquarters of the Directorate of Restoration of Old Havana, it's open to the public and has free exhibitions. Go on in; its charming patio overflowing with green plants, and the noble rooms on the first floor, with their blue wooden frames and antique furniture, offer a lovely vision of the nobility of Havana's oldest residences.

A stone's throw from the cathedral, on Calle Empedrado between Cuba and San Ignacio, is Hemingway favorite **Bodeguita del Medio** (*p. 71*) —always fun and full. While waiting for a seat, enter the house at no. 215: the **Casa de la Condesa de la Reunión,** a former private mansion built around 1820, now the **Centro de Promoción Cultural Alejo Carpentier** (*Mon-Fri 8am-4pm - donations welcome*). Around the patio, a modest exhibition, consisting of a few photographs and souvenirs, is dedicated to the life of Carpentier, a lauded Cuban author, and in particular to his book *Explosion in a Cathedral* (in Spanish, *El Siglo de Las Luces - The Century of Lights*). Practically opposite Bodeguita del Medio is the **Centro de Arte Contemporáneo Wifredo Lam** (☎ 7-861-2096 - www.wlam.cult.cu - San Ignacio at Empedrado - Tues-Sat 10am-5pm - free). It doesn't show works by Lam, the great Cuban surrealist painter, but rather temporary exhibitions of contemporary artists. A nice place to see modern Cuban artwork.

CALLE MERCADERES★★

Map III-A1-2, B2
Linking Plaza de la Catedral in the north to Plaza Vieja in the south, Calle Mercaderes forms the main artery

Farmacia y Droguería Taquechel

of Habana Vieja, a real beating heart drawing an uninterrupted flow of tourists. Beautifully renovated, it's lined in the most delightful examples of colonial houses transformed into museums, exhibition halls and galleries: each doorstep invites you to make a discovery!

The street was built to the east of the cathedral, at the crossroads of Tacón and Empedrado. After a few meters, you'll discover a long **mural fresco**: the work, by Andrés Carrillo, depicts with photographic precision 67 famous men and women from Cuban history; it was completed in 2000. After walking along the back facade of the **Palacio de los Capitanes Generales** (p. 14), you'll cross Calle Obispo. Don't miss no. 155 on this street: **Farmacia y Droguería Taquechel★★** (9am-5pm - donations welcome). This historic pharmacy, with its handsome old chandeliers, has magnificent wooden shelves filled with porcelain jars and glass bottles, among other ancient objects related to the pharmacy. This superb space, the envy of Hollywood set designers, takes you back in time.

◗ To return to Calle Mercaderes, pass the **Ambos Mundos Hotel** ("of two worlds"), a mythical establishment where Ernest Hemingway lived between 1932 and 1940 (see Where to Stay p. 86). The large ground floor café, which opens wide onto the street, offers a suggestive colonial setting for a drink, and you can also go up to the bar-restaurant on the top floor to admire the expansive view of the city and sea.

24

© Marco Lissoni/Shutterstock

A few buildings down Calle Mercaderes, at no. 114, admire the wonderful **Maqueta de la Habana Vieja★** (✐ [7] 866 4425 - 9am-6:30pm - 1,50 CUC), which reproduces in miniature the entire old town down to its smallest details. The cluster of small, colorful houses, represented at a scale of 1:500 on nearly 50 m², is a nice place to take kids 👪. At no. 120, the small **Museo del Tabaco** (Tobacco Museum) is quaint.

◖ *Continue up to the corner of Calle Obrapía.*

CASA DE LA OBRAPÍA★

Map III-A2
Enter at Calle Obrapía 158 near Mercaderes - ✐ (7) 861 3097 - 9am-5pm- free admission.
This is one of the most beautiful historical residences in Old Havana, unmistakable with its high, bright yellow and blue facade, as well as its magnificent, highly elaborate Baroque porch. Its name, "pious work", is due to its function as an orphanage in the 17C. It now houses a varied collection (tools, 19C furniture, exhibitions of contemporary works, etc.). Walk through the galleries and corridors of its large rooms, with their unique historical character, and out on the beautiful patio.
On leaving, you'll discover the **Casa de África** (*Calle Obrapía 157*), the first of many small museums set up around the house, in various old buildings, in order to showcase the donations that Fidel Castro received from different countries and whole continents.

At the corner of calles Obrapía and Mercaderes *(no. 156)* you'll run into the **Casa de México** (✐[7] 861 8166 - Tues-Sat 9am-2:30pm - free admission), featuring a collection of Mexican ceramics, frescoes, and portraits, including those of Fidel and Raúl Castro; a little farther down the same street *(no. 111)* is the **Casa de Asia**. Admire the **Casa Oswaldo Guayasamín**, dedicated to the prolific Ecuadorian artist and regularly presenting contemporary exhibitions *(see p. 68)*.

Just after the small Parque Guayasamín, a pleasant island of greenery created on a former wasteland, is the **Museo de la Armería** (✐ Mon 1pm-5pm, Tues-Sat 9am-4:45pm - free admission, donations welcome). This beautiful historical armory, open to calle Mercaderes, was looted by Havana students during the 1959 revolution. The collection of antique weapons is worth a look. At the next junction with Calle Lamparilla is Hotel Conde de Villanueva *(see Where to stay, p. 86)*, whose cigar shop is popular with enthusiasts *(see Shopping, p 78.)*.

Just down the road, at the corner of Calle Amargura, is the **Museo de la Cerámica** (✐7-861-6130 - Tues-Sat 9am-5pm, Sun 9am-1pm - 1 CUC), located in the **Casa Aguilera**, a beautiful colonial setting for the exhibition of works that are realistic, dreamlike, conceptual, pictorial or sensual. Among them, you can admire those of the most important Cuban ceramists of the 20C, such as Wifredo Lam and Amelia Peláez.

25

Hemingway in Havana

From 1932 to 1940, the famous American writer occupied room 511 of the Ambos Mundos Hotel, writing in his modest room his novel For Whom The Bell Tolls. When his war wounds bothered him, Hemingway would go to neighborhood bars in search of moral and physical comfort. His nocturnal wanderings always began with El Floridita, at the corner of Avenida de Bélgica and Calle Obispo (see p. 64). After a few daiquiris or "papa's special" (with double measures of rum), he would go down the street to the Plaza de la Catedral (p. 21). A few steps away, he would sit with a mojito in the Bodeguita del Medio (p. 64). Soothed, he would reach the port from where he would cast off to do some fishing worthy of The Old Man and The Sea.

Finally, on the other side of Calle Amargura, there is a small gourmet institution in Havana: the **Museo del Chocolate** *(see Where to snack, p. 63),* a must for enjoying a good hot or cold chocolate.

26

▷ *At the next intersection, Calle Mercaderes leads to Plaza Vieja.*

PLAZA VIEJA★★★

Map II-C3
Colorful, lively and full of character, Plaza Vieja ("Old Square") is, as its name suggests, one of the oldest in the city. Ocher, blue or green plaster, multiple stained glass windows with shimmering geometric motifs (a superb spectacle at night when the interiors are lit) and balconies with elaborate ironwork. Such is the intact charm of this large esplanade erected during the second half of the 16C, when it was then called Plaza Nueva, the "New Square"!
If the Plaza de Armas was reserved for military exercises, the Plaza Vieja was intended for civilians: it hosted a slave market and then a covered market. It was demolished at the beginning of the 20C, before being transformed as often as not into a large car park. Today, beautifully restored and pedestrianized, it's one of the jewels of the tourist district. All the buildings in Plaza Vieja now house cultural institutions, museums, galleries and cafés-restaurants. Before going around, you can climb up to the top of the **Edificio Gómez Vila**, whose rich Belle Epoque architecture dominates the corner of calles Mercaderes and Brasil.
The top floor houses a **Camera Obscura** ▲▲ *(on the 8th floor, access by elevator - 9:30am-5pm - 2CUC),* a curiosity that optical enthusiasts will appreciate: in a small, all-black room, there is a 1.80m diameter dome on which the panorama of the city is projected, filtered by a periscope installed just above, at 35m high. The vision of the city, very detailed (you can see pedestrians walking in the nearby streets), does not fail to impress. The adjacent terrace offers a beautiful view, this time very real, of the Plaza Vieja.

Continuing clockwise in the square, discover a pretty blue house; dating from 1752, it houses the **Fototeca de Cuba** *(Tues-Sat 10am-5:30pm - free admission)*, which presents photographic exhibitions, often by great Cuban names; do not hesitate to ask for information.

Immediately afterwards appears the retro facade of the former **Cine Habana**, now transformed into a **planetarium** 👥. Now a must for Havana schoolchildren, the show traces the history of the universe from the Big Bang *(in Spanish - Wed-Sat 9:30am-5:30pm - 10 CUC)*.

A little farther on, after the retro decor of coffee-lovers' favorite El Escorial *(see Where to snack, p. 74)*, stands at the corner of calles Muralla and Inquisidor a wonderful example of Art Nouveau, richly sculpted: the former **Vienna Hotel** (1906), which, after having been longinhabited by Cuban families, is completely restored. At its feet, the first house on the south side of Plaza Vieja houses the modest **Museo del Naipe**, dedicated to the history of the playing card *(☎7 860 1534 - open every day but Mon 9am-6pm - free)*.

At the corner of calles Muralla and San Ignacio stands one of the oldest buildings in the square: preceded by a beautiful stone colonnade, the **Casa del Conde de Jaruco**★ was built in 1737. Today it's the headquarters of the **Fondo de Bienes Culturales** and has art and craft shops. On the other side of the crossing, the yellow facade of **Factoria Plaza Vieja** houses a brewery *(see Where to drink, p. 64)* and is a favorite people-watching spot.

Two buildings farther up, you can take a look at the **Vitrina de Valonia**, an unexpected center for the cultural promotion of Wallonia, where exhibitions of Belgian comic strips sometimes take place.

Finally, at the corner of calles Brasil and San Ignacio, **Casa de las Hermanas Cárdenas** bears the name of the two sisters who had it built at the end of the 18C. This small ocher building became the headquarters of the Philharmonic Society of the city in 1824 before being transformed into **Centro de Desarollo de las Artes Visuales** (Visual Arts Development Center), regularly presenting the work of contemporary artists.

◗ *Go up Calle Brasil to the east to reach Plaza de San Francisco de Asís.*

PLAZA DE SAN FRANCISCO ★

Map II-C3

Bordering the historic center, this vast square next to the bay is often swept by a strong wind: greatly eroded, the statues of the pretty church of Saint Francis of Assisi to which it owes its name seem to have become salt sculptures! In the center of the esplanade, the beautiful marble Fuente de los Leones (Lion Fountain) was sculpted by the Italian artist Gaggini and erected in 1836. From 1844 onwards, it was moved around to several parts of the city and did not return to its original location until 1963. While the Plaza de San Francisco de Asís was built at the end of the 16C, the commercial buildings surrounding it—the former Lonja del

Basilica Menor de San Francisco de Asís, Plaza de San Francisco de Asís

© Claire Boobbyer/Michelin

Commercio (Trade Exchange) in the north or the customs office in the east—date only to the beginning of the 20C.

BASILICA MENOR DE SAN FRANCISCO DE ASIS★★

Map II-C3
Calle Oficios between Amargura and Muralla - Mon-Sat 9:50am-5pm - 2 CUC.
These buildings have a turbulent history. The project to build the Franciscan monastery dates back to 1570, but work did not begin until ten years later. Completed in 1591, the church had a significant religious and cultural influence in Latin America. Between 1719 and 1733, the monastery and the church had to be rebuilt, as they showed signs of decay. Then in 1842, laws on the dismantling of clergy property marked the end of this religious building, which was converted into a warehouse. Finally, four years later, a cyclone destroyed the choir, which was replaced by a tromp-d'oeil.

Since 1990, this religious complex has aroused renewed interest and has been the subject of major restoration work. You can attend renowned classical music **concerts** in the spacious and uncluttered nave of the church (*every Saturday at 6pm - 10*

CUC). Ivory and silverware are on display in the nave, while the ground floor of the cloister houses a model of the convent and liturgical objects. From the cloister floor, visitors can access the **coro alto (rood screen)**. From there, a steep staircase leads to the top of the bell tower, with an unobstructed **view★** of the whole city and the old **Loja del Comercio** (1907-1909), just opposite.

COCHE MAMBÍ

Map II-C3
Calle Churruca - Tue 9:30am-4:30pm, Sun 9:30am - 2pm - free.
Going down to the docks isCcalle Churruca, which shelters a real curiosity: the alley is almost entirely occupied by a railway carriage! This former presidential carriage has retained all the luxury of yesteryear: the bedroom, lounge, dining room and kitchen look just as they did in the early 20C.
Steps away, on Avenida del Puerto, is the **Museo del Ron Havana Club** *(www.havanaclubmuseum.com - Mon-Thur 9am-5:30pm, Friday-Sunday 9am-4:30pm - 7 CUC, 25min guided tour in English).* The small museum on the first floor explains the stages of rum making, but the visit is above all an excuse for tasting and selling! The bar is open until midnight.

❍ *Enter Habana Vieja again by going up Calle Sol to the convent of Santa Clara.*

The Ceiba Tree
Also known as the kapok, or cotton, tree, the ceiba [pronounced SAY-bah] is a large tropical tree in the same family as the African baobab. Among the tallest in a tropical forest, the ceiba can grow as high as 60m/197ft. It's distinguished by its umbrella-shaped canopy and thick, cylindrical trunk (up to 3.5m/12ft or more in circumference). The tree's sizable above-ground roots resemble buttresses. Pollinated in part by bats, ceibas flower and bear fruit when their leaves fall off.

SOUTHERN HABANA VIEJA

Map II
Allow 1.5 hours
Young people play baseball, overloaded bicycles skirt around ancient cars and pedestrians at high speed, the discussions between neighbors from balcony to balcony barely drown out the latest hit songs, played at full volume on ancient radios...Such is the spectacle offered by these popular streets! As much as the north of Habana Vieja has something of a museum quality, the rest of the district—from the train station to Calle Obispo—remains thoroughly alive. Tourists venture here in smaller numbers, but more should: it's remarkable. Everywhere, dust-covered, once-charming buildings in the process of decay (ironwork gnawed at by rust, sculptures overgrown by weeds) sit

on bumpy pavement and sometimes house humble shops. It's a setting that betrays harsh living conditions, but one that bursts with life. Clothes dry hung from the smallest window, children run from all sides, and everyone does an infinite amount of light housework in the middle of the streets; the line between public and private is delightfully blurry. Here is a teenage girl applying nail polish, there an amateur electrician scratching his head in front of an impressive array of cables. Small scenes that seem inconsequential on the surface actually say a lot, especially about family solidarity, a real sense of community and resourcefulness!

☺ **Good to know** – Due to a lack of resources and consequently of maintenance, the neighborhood's heritage suffers and many buildings are now closed to the public, awaiting hypothetical renovations. To explore in the company of a guide, sign up for one of the interesting tours offered by San Cristobal Agency (*see www.cubaheritage.com/san-cristobal-description.htm*).

IGLESIA Y CONVENTO DE SANTA CLARA★

Map II-B3
Calle Cuba between Sol and Luz - closed for ongoing renovations. Completed in 1644 after six years of construction, Santa Clara was nevertheless Cuba's first monastery for nuns. Surrounding construction at the beginning of the 20C, putting an end to their privacy,

forced the sisters to move. The convent was sold in 1919 to a public works company, then became the headquarters of the National Centre for Conservation, Restoration and Museology, transforming the former nuns' quarters into workshops for the restoration of textiles, furniture, paintings and statues. All that remains is for the building itself to be renovated so that the superb **cloister★★**—cooled by the **Fuente de la Samaritana**, the city's first fountain, installed in the 17C—as well as the original woodwork that adorns the walls, can be rediscovered.

In the same street, at the corner of Calle Acosta, stands the sober gray stone facade of Havana's oldest church, the **Espíritu Santo Church** (*Tues-Sat 9am-12pm, 3pm-5pm, Sun 9am-12pm*). Built in 1632 by a group of freed slaves, it was the second parish church after the one that stood on the site of the Palacio de las Capitanes Generales. The left nave and facade were added in the second half of the 18C. Inside, the dark wood of the altarpieces and the choir framework contrasts with the light stone of the nave walls and the vaults of the choir.

◗ *Go down two blocks to Calle Merced.*

IGLESIA Y CONVENTO DE NUESTRA SEÑORA DE LA MERCED★

Map II-C4
Corner of Calles Cuba and Merced. This architectural complex was started in 1755 but was completed only in the following century. The

church has benefited from a rich decorative agenda: polychrome sculptures, altarpieces and very elaborate **sacristy furniture★**, and many **frescoes★**, especially on the dome. The effects of time are visible, but the whole is all the more poetic. Practically opposite Nuestra Señora de la Merced, at Calle Cuba no. 815, is **Boxeo Rafael Trejo's Gimnasio**, an open-air ring where, especially on Saturday mornings, fans of Cuban boxer Kid Chocolate compete against each other. You're guaranteed a uniquely Cuban atmosphere in this small institution.

◗ *Turn left into Calle Leonor Pérez (Paula).*

Built between 1730 and 1745, the **Church of San Francisco de Paula★** stands on a small square overlooking the bay. The enclosure also included a women's hospital, which was destroyed in 1946, as was the church choir. The rest of the building, including its beautiful **dome★**, was spared and recently restored. Farther up, on the Desamparados quay, next to the San Francisco church, is vast renovated warehouse **Nave San José**, which houses a number of small craft shops selling souvenirs of all kinds *(see Shopping, p.78)*. Next door, the **Antiguo Almacén de la Madera y el Tabaco**, a warehouse where wood and tobacco were stored, is now home to a brewery. There is hope that the entire sector near the port will benefit from the same renovation effort.

◗ *Take Calle Cuba to return to Calle Leonor Pérez (Paula).*

CASA NATAL DE JOSÉ MARTÍ★

Map II-B4
Calle Leonor Pérez (Paula) 314 btwn Picota and Egido - ☏ *(7) 861 3778 - open Tues 9:15am-5:45pm, Sun 9:15am-12:45pm - 2 CUC.*
"The Apostle of Cuban Independence" was born on 28 January 1853 in this small house and spent the first four years of his life there. In this museum, inaugurated in 1925, are some of Marti's personal objects, closely linked to the island's history. Among the photographs is one of note: in it, Marti holds his son on his knees, a smile on his face. Also on display is the only known portrait of him, painted by the Swedish painter Hermann Norman in 1891. When you reach Avenida Egido, you'll discover the imposing railway station (under renovation), built at the beginning of the 20C. On either side are the remains of an arsenal and old **fortifications** *(muralla)*, demolished in 1863.

◗ *Go up Avenida Egido to the right. Leave the station on your left and turn right into Calle Acosta, just behind the Puerto de Sagua restaurant.*

In Calle Acosta, you'll pass under a Baroque arch, the **Arco de Belén** (Bethlehem Arch), built in 1772 to connect the convent of the same name to the houses on the other side of the street.

To Criss-Cross Havana in an Old American

*With their magnificent curves and shiny bodies in bold colors (hot pink, apple green, cerulean blue), Chevrolets, Cadillacs, and other 1950s classic cars have become emblematic of Havana (and Cuba). Cared for lovingly by their owners, they have been restored to their original condition. In the context of the US embargo, which severely restricted the import of new cars, these classic cars have become a source of wealth, to the point that the State prohibits their resale abroad. The most beautiful convertibles give rides to tourists, who embark on wild tours of the city. Most of these cars park in front of the **Gran Teatro** (p. 34, Map II-A3) and, in the north of Old Havana, on the Parque Céspedes (Map II-B2): expect to pay **30-40 CUC for a one-hour or 90-minute tour** that will take you out to Vedado and Miramar, with an essential drive along the Malecón, the wind in your hair. Another option that is much cheaper and no less picturesque is a trip in a **collective taxi** (see p. 93), most often a buzzing and patched-up Chevrolet where several people crowd together. Without a shock absorber, the journey can be bumpy!*

◗ *Just after the arch, turn left onto Calle Compostela.*

IGLESIA Y CONVENTO DE NUESTRA SEÑORA DE BELÉN★

Map II-B4

Calle Compostela between Luz and Acosta - church closed for restoration.
This vast complex, freshly painted yellow, was built between 1712 and 1718 for the Bethlehem congregation and was the first Baroque building in Havana. In 1856, it passed into the hands of the Jesuits and then became one of the premises of the Academy of Sciences. Abandoned since 1925 and seriously damaged by a fire in 1991, the church and convent are gradually recovering their splendor thanks to a restoration still in progress. The convent returned to its first charitable functions by hosting a retirement home and a center for handicapped children.

◗ *Walk up Compostela for three blocks, to Teniente Rey (Calle Brasil).*

MUSEO DE LA FARMACIA HABANERA★

Map II-B3

Corner of Calles Brasil (Tiente Rey) and Compostela - ✆(7) 866 7556 - Tues-Sat 9am-5pm - free but donations welcome.
Located in the former Droguería Sarrá—opened by Dr José Sarra at the end of the 19C—this museum, inaugurated in 2004, revives a former Cuban pharmacy. In the succession of large rooms, the walls are decorated with magnificent carved wooden displays containing many vials once intended for pharmaceutical preparations. You can also admire

many 19C and 20C objects: scales, vials, jars found during archaeological excavations in Old Havana. In this shop, where all decor is intact, time appears to have stood still.

◗ *Walk up Calle Brasil (Teniente Rey) for two blocks towards the Capitol.*

Make a small right turn at church **Santo Cristo del Buen Viaje**. While the first buildings were built in 1640, the current church was built in 1755: its red tiled roof and elaborate facade framed by two white towers form a pretty picture. The square, beloved by the inhabitants of the district, offers many picturesque scenes at any time of the day.

FROM EL CAPITOLIO TO PASEO DEL PRADO

Map II
Allow one day if you visit all the museums.
At the end of the lanes of Habana Vieja the monumental Capitol (El Capitolio) creates a surprising break in scale. This is where Havana becomes a true capital. The area around Parque Central, a vast esplanade, was the city's showcase during the Belle Epoque: wide avenues favorable to car traffic, a large theater, lush promenade Paseo del Prado, museums, luxury hotels and Parisian-style cafés. This was the favorite territory of American mobsters in the first half of the 20C. Today, although decayed, the area remains suggestive of a bygone era; its traffic jams of gleaming old American cars create a dynamic atmosphere you won't find anywhere else.

EL CAPITOLIO★★

Map II-A3
Open but under renovation.
A relic of the American era, this replica of the Capitol in Washington, D.C.—itself inspired by the Paris Pantheon—was completed in 1929 under Machado's presidency and remained the seat of Parliament until the revolution.
The main entrance leads directly under the dome, where there is a 17.5m-high, 49-tonne **gilded bronze statue** cast in Italy by the sculptor Angelo Zanelli and representing the Republic. In the ground below this rotunda is embedded a **diamond** marking km 0 from which all the distances on the island are calculated. An immense hallway with exceptional acoustics leads to the various rooms of the Capitol. Before the restoration work currently under way, it was possible to visit the chamber where parliamentarians met, as well as the various offices and conference rooms. Beautiful frescoes decorate the walls and ceiling of the Martí lounge. Admire the precious woods of the **National Library of Science and Technology★**.

PARQUE CENTRAL★

Map II-A3
Under the shade of its palm trees, Cubans gather at any time of the day to discuss baseball, bet on

33

their favorite team, or simply enjoy the tranquility of the place. In the center is a **statue of José Martí.** The sculpture to the glory of the "Apostle of Independence" was made by the Cuban Vilalta de Saavedra in 1904.

GRAN TEATRO DE LA HABANA★

Map II-A3
www.balletcuba.cult.cu - guided tour Tues 9am-5pm, Sun 9am-1pm - Tours 5 CUC (performance tickets around 30 CUC).
Between Calles San José and San Rafael stands the imposing silhouette of this theater, where operas, concerts and performances of the Cuban National Ballet—founded in 1948 by

Buildings on Paseo del Prado
© Claire Boobbyer/Michelin

Alicia Alonso, who became one of the emblematic figures of the Cuban revolution— are performed.
Attached to the former Teatro Tacón, which was built in 1838, the current building was completed in 1915 to house the Galician Social Club. Its superb neo-Baroque facade has been restored to its former glory: the many white marble balustrades, statues and sculptures—including, at each corner of the building, an angel seemingly taking flight from one of the turrets— create an exemplary architectural work of the Belle Epoque.
The interior has also recovered its luster, in particular the large Italian-style hall, where countless artists have performed, from operatic tenor Enrico Caruso to British pop band Simply Red. The marble **staircase★**, wrapped around a mosaic, is a marvel of elegance.
Next door is the **Hotel Inglaterra**, a Neoclassical building classified as a National Monument. The establishment *(see "Where to stay" p. 75)* houses the **Café El Louvre**, a popular meeting place under its arcades. In the 19C, groups of young people who were hostile to the colonial government liked to meet or discuss issues on the sidewalk, known as the *acera del Louvre* ("Louvre sidewalk"). On 27 November 1871, Nicolás Estévanez, a Spanish soldier, broke his sword at this place and gave up his career in protest against the execution of eight independence medical students. In homage to these students, a memorial was erected at the other end of the Prado, at the entrance to the bay.

At the corner of Avenida Zulueta and Calle San Rafael, east of the square, **Manzana de Gómez** is unlikely to go unnoticed. The imposing 19C building, enlarged in 1910, occupies a whole block. The historic department store is currently undergoing major renovation. On the other side of Calle San Rafael stands the National Museum of Fine Arts.

MUSEO NACIONAL DE BELLAS ARTES★

Map II-A2
Calle Obispo between Agramonte and Bélgica - ☎ (7) 862 01 40 or 861 38 56 - www.bellasartes.co.cu - Tues-Fri 10am-6pm, Sat 10am-9pm, Sun 9am-1pm - 5 CUC, 8 CUC ticket combined with the Museo de Arte Cubano (see p. 36).

This large museum occupies the former **Centro Asturiano**, a building designed by Spanish architect Manuel del Busto and inaugurated in 1928. It offers an airy museo-graphic space to its collections covering more than two millennia of art history, based on works from **Antiquity★**: Greek statuettes, Roman mosaics, Coptic fabrics, Egyptian talismans and funeral vases, as well as Sumerian tablets (level 4).

In addition to interesting **religious paintings from South America** and the **United States** (17-19C), the main centers of European art are represented. The **Spanish art rooms★★** (level 3) impress with works by Huguet (15C), Ribera (17C), Fortuny (19C), and many paintings by Sorolla (20C); a space is also dedicated to Eugénio Lucas Velázquez (19C), one of the best followers of Goya art. Level 4 houses **French art★★**, including the impressive **Procession of Forgiveness in Brittany** by Jules Breton (19C), a **Portrait of a Young Woman** by Greuze (18C), a very kitsch allegory of the sunset (*Atardecer*) by Bouguereau (19C), and **The Wave** by Courbet (19C). The last level presents works from German schools (*Crucifixion* from the school of Lucas Cranach the Elder in the 16C), **Flemish** in the 17C, (Brueghel de Velours and Van Dyck), 18C **English** (portraits of Gainsborough and Reynolds, Hoppner), and especially **Italian★**: take the time to discover **Reception of the Legate of Carpaccio** (16C), a beautiful Guardi (18C) and a Canaletto from the English period (18C).

❯ *Cross over Parque Central to Paseo del Prado.*

PASEO DEL PRADO (PASEO DE MARTÍ)★

Map II-A1-2
The once very chic Prado (Paseo de Martí) promenade stretches from the northwest of Parque Central to the seaside. This area is home to some of the city's largest museums.

Once a mecca for the Cuban aristocracy, the Prado is lined with opulent buildings, some of which, perfectly rococo, crumble under stucco and architectural flourishes. Sadly most have had their facades gnawed away by time. Walking down the boulevard—dotted with wrought iron streetlights and marble benches of another age, and shaded by a few scattered laurels—has something nostalgic about it.

▶ *Join Avenida Bélgica, parallel to the Prado.*

At the corner of Avenida Bélgica and Calle Progreso, the ocher facade of the **Edificio Bacardía** stands out from the surrounding buildings. This impressive ceramic-covered Art Deco building was built in the late 1920s for Emilio Bacardí, the wealthy owner of sugar cane plantations and the famous rum distillery of the same name. The bat that can be seen at the top of the tower is found on rum bottles; on a building of this style, it brings to mind Gotham City and Batman. Give a small tip to the guard and you can ask to go up to discover the superb view of the city.

MUSEO NACIONAL DE BELLAS ARTES-ARTE CUBANO★★

Map II-A2
Calle Trocadero between Zulueta and Bélgica - same opening hours as the Museo Nacional de Bellas Artes - 5 CUC, 8 CUC combined ticket with the main part of the museum (see p. 35)
This austere 1950s construction houses the Cuban arts collection of the Museum of Fine Arts. It's certainly the most interesting museum in the city. In a beautiful three-level space you'll discover a wide range of national works from the 16C to the present day, as well as a sculpture garden. A visit is a special opportunity to appreciate the astonishing vitality of Cuban painting in the 20C, with artists of the 1930s influenced by Gauguin, such as Antonio Gattorno or Víctor Manuel García Valdés (his **La Gitana Tropical** was nicknamed the "American Mona Lisa"!). Marcelo Pogolotti and, a little later, Roberto Diago showed themselves sensitive to surrealism. In the 1950s and 60s, many artists became the apostles of the Cuban Revolution, while adopting styles that went as far as abstraction. Servando Cabrera Moreno (**Milicias Campesinas**) and Raúl Martínez (**26 de Julio**) are among the most important. Finally,

© Claire Boobbyer/Michelin

Museo de Bellas Artes-Arte Cubano

the museum dedicates an entire room to the most illustrious painter in the country: Wifredo Lam, whose **Huracán**, **The Third World**, and the magnificent **Portrait of Eulalia Soliño** are displayed in the **cambio de siglo** section (1894-1927).

As you leave, take a look at the beautiful Moorish facade of the Hotel Sevilla *(Calle Trocadero 55, on the other side of Calle Zulueta)*.

MUSEO DE LA REVOLUCIÓN★

Map II-A12
Calle Refugio btwn Zulueta and Bélgica - ☎ (7) 862 40 91/98 - 10am-5pm - 8 CUC - some rooms, under renovation, are closed.
A symbolic building: the 1959 Revolution Museum took over the former **Palacio Presidencial★**, built in 1913. It became the residence of the presidents of the Republic in 1920. The museum traces the history of Cuba from the colonial period to the revolution, in a profusion of photographs, objects and documents. It reflects and stimulates the sense of national pride felt by Cubans, many of whom visit it. However, dated pieces, information in Spanish only in the form of propaganda, the large number of visitors and the cramped nature of the rooms—not to mention the relatively high price of admission—could put off those who are not particularly interested in Cuban history. That said, is interior is sumptuous, decorated in part by American jewelry company Tiffany & Co., and as photos *are* allowed

inside (no flash) you can snap some of the building's beautiful ceilings and scrollwork.

Outside, visible from the street, stands the **Granma Memorial**. Fidel Castro, accompanied by 81 companions, landed on the coast of Santiago de Cuba in 1956 aboard this 20-metre-long boat, which sits in the middle of a glass pavilion. Around the memorial are the weapons of the revolutionary struggle, such as the truck that attacked the presidential palace on March 13, 1957 and an aircraft used during the Bay of Pigs Invasion.

CASA DE PÉREZ DE LA RIVA★

Map II-B2.
At the meeting point of Avenida de las Misiones and Calle Cárcel, an Italian Renaissance facade hits an anachronistic note next to the expressways of the Parque de los Mártires. This elegant house from 1905 is now the Museo **Nacional de la Música**. This national music museum presents an eclectic collection of Cuban and foreign instruments, where pianos, Indian zithras, Haitian drums, Russian balalaikas, music boxes, photos of musicians, and scores all come together.
In front of the museum, towards the sea, an imposing **statue of General Máximo Gómez** is erected in honor of the hero of the wars of independence. On the left is the **monument dedicated to medical students** shot by the Spanish in 1871.

Centro Habana

The municipio of Centro Habana remains largely untouristed despite its strategic location between Habana Vieja and Vedado. This district, bordered to the south by the Arroyo Avenue (Manglar), extends from the west of Paseo de Martí (Prado) to Vedado and opens to the north on the Gulf of Mexico. Far from the buzzing of La Rampa, let yourself be seduced by Cuban nonchalance in the narrow streets lined with two- or three-story buildings, where there are many vendors and entrepreneurs—hair dressers, the refiller of lighters, mechanics—setting up shop on the sidewalk. Even in these square urban blocks it's not impossible to see a hen followed by its chicks, an amazing sight in the heart of a capital city. Centro will become a favorite for lovers of authentic street scenes.

▶**Access:** As with most of Havana, this area is best explored on foot.
Area map: ***Map IV***. Detachable map.
▶**Tips:** Because there are fewer tourists here, there can be occasional petty crime at night. Although the police are very present, don't walk around with valuables and avoid dark alleyways with little traffic.

BARRIO CHINO

Map IV-C2.

Havana's Chinatown occupies the few streets that extend between Calle Zanja and Avenida Simón Bolívar (Reina), where a monumental gate typical of a **chinatown** stands. In the second half of the 19C, more than 120,000 Chinese immigrated to Cuba to replace the revolting slaves. Some members of this community later settled in this part of Havana, however today almost no Chinese live in Barrio Chino. Traveling vendors offer East Asian dishes at the **agromercado**, a small farmers' market located at the corner of Calles Zanja and Rayo (prices are low, but you'll need to pay in CUP, not CUC).

⬤ *Go down Calle Rayo or one of the streets parallel to Avenida Reina/ Simón Bolívar.*

Farther on, you'll find yourself on Avenida Salvador Allende (formerly Carlos III and still called this by locals) which leads straight to the Vedado. Explore the neighborhood, imagining it as it used to be and taking in the beautiful if sadly decaying buildings. Sometimes—at the end of one of the streets leading to the ocean, between two rows of buildings—a huge spray of sea hangs in the air before crashing down on the Malecón. Catch it with your camera if you can.

CALLEJON DE HAMEL★

Map IV-B2

Between Calles Aramburu and Hospital, near San Lázaro.
Here paints and lives Salvador González Escalona, whom the inhabitants simply called "Salvador". Cayo Hueso is a mini neighborhood

Callejón de Hamel

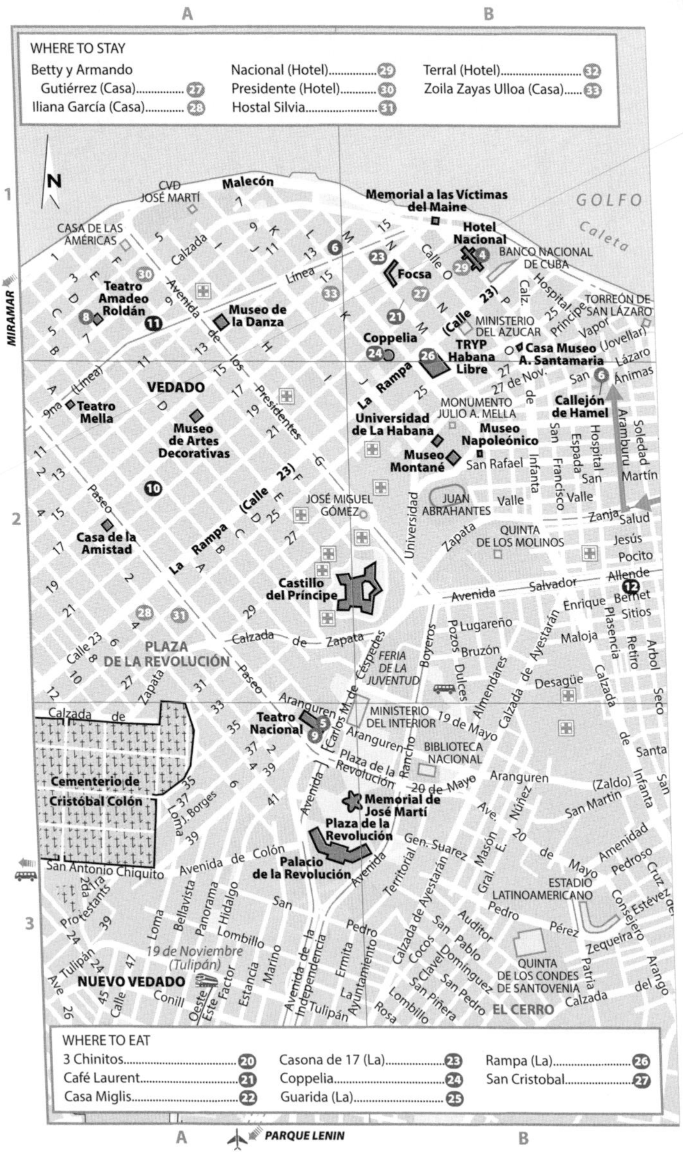

Map labels

N

CVD JOSÉ MARTÍ

Malecón

Memorial a las Víctimas del Maine

Hotel Nacional

GOLFO

Caleta

CASA DE LAS AMÉRICAS

Calzada

Línea

Calle

Calle 23

BANCO NACIONAL DE CUBA

MINISTERIO DEL AZUCAR

TORREÓN DE SAN LÁZARO

MIRAMAR

Teatro Amadeo Roldán

Museo de la Danza

Focsa

Coppelia

La Rampa

TRYP Habana Libre

Casa Museo A. Santamaria

27 de Nov.

Callejón de Hamel

VEDADO

Teatro Mella

Museo de Artes Decorativas

Universidad de La Habana

MONUMENTO JULIO A. MELLA

Museo Napoleónico

Museo Montané

San Rafael

Infante

La Rampa

Calle 23

JOSÉ MIGUEL GÓMEZ

Universidad

Zapata

JUAN ABRAHANTES

QUINTA DE LOS MOLINOS

Salud

Casa de la Amistad

Castillo del Príncipe

Avenida Salvador

Calzada de Zapata

FERIA DE LA JUVENTUD

PLAZA DE LA REVOLUCIÓN

Teatro Nacional

MINISTERIO DEL INTERIOR

19 de Mayo

BIBLIOTECA NACIONAL

Cementerio de Cristóbal Colón

Plaza de la Revolución

Memorial de José Martí

Plaza de la Revolución

Palacio de la Revolución

San Antonio Chiquito

ESTADIO LATINOAMERICANO

QUINTA DE LOS CONDES DE SANTOVENIA

EL CERRO

19 de Noviembre (Tulipán)

NUEVO VEDADO

40

PARQUE LENIN

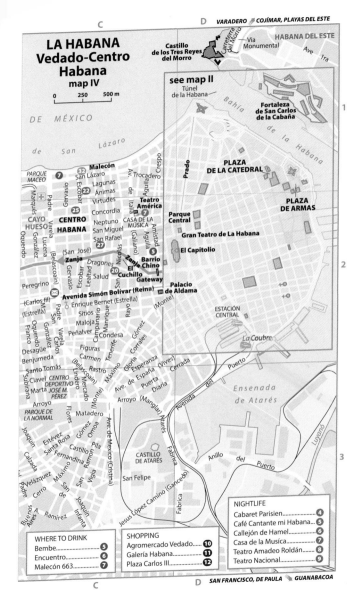

LA HABANA
Vedado-Centro Habana
map IV

0 — 250 — 500 m

VARADERO · **COJÍMAR, PLAYAS DEL ESTE**

HABANA DEL ESTE

Ave. 1ra

Vía Monumental

Carretera del Morro

Castillo de los Tres Reyes del Morro

D

C

see map II

Túnel de la Habana

Bahía

de la Habana

Fortaleza de San Carlos de la Cabaña

1

DE MÉXICO

de San Lázaro

PARQUE MACEO ❼

Malecón
San Lázaro ㉒
Lagunas
Ánimas
Virtudes
Concordia

Av. Trocadero
Crespo
de Italia
Aguila

Prado

PLAZA DE LA CATEDRAL

PLAZA DE ARMAS

Marqués
Padre
Gervasio
Escobar

CAYO HUESO

CENTRO HABANA

㉒
㉕

Teatro América ❼

CASA DE LA MÚSICA

Neptuno
San Miguel
San Rafael

Amistad
Aguila
(Galiano)

Parque Central

Gran Teatro de La Habana

❷❼

Lucena
Varela
González
Oquendo

(San José)
Zanja
Dragones
Salud

Escobar
Lealtad
Nicolás

El Capitolio

Barrio Chino
❺
Zanja El Cuchillo ⑳
Gateway

Palacio de Aldama

ESTACIÓN CENTRAL

Peregrino
Gervasio

(Belascoaín)

Avenida Simón Bolívar (Reina)

(Carlos III)
(Estrella)

M

❆ Enrique Bernet (Estrella)
Sitios
Maloja
Condesa
Figuras
Carmen

Padre
San
Campanario
Manrique
Tenerife
Máximo

Rayo
Gómez
Corrales
Gloria
Esperanza

(Monte)

La Coubre

Oquendo
Franco
Desagüe
Benjumeda
Santo Tomás
Subirana
Marta

González
Varela
Carlos
(Belascoaín)
Lindero
Rastro
Mercado

CENTRO DEPORTIVO JOSÉ M. PÉREZ

(Vives)
Ave. de España
Puerta
Diaria
Cerrada

Ensenada de Atarés

Arroyo
PARQUE DE LA NORMAL
Joaquín
Estévez
Santa Rosa
Fernandina
Calzada

Flores
Gómez
Omoa
Castillo
San Ramón

Arroyo (Manglar)
Matadero
Maravés

Ave. de México (Cristina)

Avenida del Puerto

Puerto

Luyanó

Velázquez
Cerro
Padre
Buenos Aires
Ramírez

Máximo
San
Joaquín
Infanta
de

Pila
Vigía
Fábrica

CASTILLO DE ATARÉS

San Felipe

Jesús López Camino (Gancedo)

Fábrica

Anillo

del Puerto

3

41

SAN FRANCISCO, DE PAULA · **GUANABACOA**

WHERE TO DRINK
Bembe.........................❺
Encuentro...................❻
Malecón 663...............❼

SHOPPING
Agromercado Vedado......❿
Galería Habana............⓫
Plaza Carlos III............⓬

NIGHTLIFE
Cabaret Parisien..................❹
Café Cantante mi Habana...❺
Callejón de Hamel...............❻
Casa de la Música...............❼
Teatro Amadeo Roldán.......❽
Teatro Nacional...................❾

in the heart of Centro Habana, and within it is Callejón de Hamel, a street like no other. One day in 1990, Salvador came to paint the wall of a friend's house and ended up **painting the whole alley** with the consent of the neighbors.

The resulting street mural is an explosion of extravagant colors and shapes. Nourished by Picasso, Dalí, Gaudí or Hundertwasser, the artist also draws his inspiration from the **santería** (see The Island's Main Religions, p.116). In addition to his paintings on walls or on canvas, Salvador cuts bathtubs in half before casting them in concrete to make public benches, assembles metal pieces to make sculptures, shapes statues...his house in the middle of the **callejón** looks like a cave. You can enter to admire some of the works and even buy some as souvenirs. The presence of a red Mercury in the street usually means that the master

is in. On Sunday afternoons, people hurry to the **callejón** to dance the rumba and enjoy the **drink El Negrón** (see Nightlife, p. 70).

REAL FÁBRICA DE TABACOS PARTAGÁS ★

Off map

Calle San Carlos 816 between Sitios and Peñalvez - Mon-Fri 9am-1pm - 10 CUC.

😊 **Good to know** – Most major hotels (ask at reception) organize guided tours of this cigar factory.

South of Centro Habana, this famous cigar factory, once located just behind the **Capitol** (see p. 33), is an excursion destination in itself. Founded in 1845, it remains one of the oldest tobacco factories in Cuba, where a real army of infinitely skilled workers roll world-famous Havanas. The guided tour lets you discover all the stages of cigar making.

THE MALECÓN ★★

Map IV-A1, B1

One of the capital city's most cherished landmarks, the **Malecón** is affectionately called **el gran sofa** ("the big sofa") by locals. All year long hundreds of residents and tourists come here night and day to while away the hours sitting on its **seawall**, taking in the scenery. The wide waterfront **boulevard** extends about 8km/5mi on Havana's northern shore, from the Castillo de San Salvador de la Punta in Habana Vieja west to the Almendares River, which separates Vedado from Miramar.

© Claire Boobbyer/Michelin

Real Fábrica de Tabacos Partagás

42

The pedestrian **sidewalk** that was built next to the six-lane coastal thoroughfare offers a microcosm of life in Havana. Here youngsters scamper up the seawall, anglers watch their lines, vendors sell cheap cigars, and lovers recline entwined as vintage American cars and coco-taxis cruise Havana's busiest east-west street.

Sunset casts an array of vivid colors on the rows of 19C and early 20C balconied buildings that line the Malecón in its Centro Habana's portion. In stormy weather, the walkway is much empiter, as heavy winds send huge waves crashing over the seawall, flooding the road and spraying the weather-beaten buildings with corrosive salt from the ocean waters. In early 2018, much of the length of the Malecón became a WiFi hotspot, making it even more popular than it already was. This is the best spot in Havana for people-watching.

Vedado★

West of Centro Habana lies the Plaza de la Revolución Municipio. Within this district, north of the Cementerio de Cristóbal Colón (Christopher Columbus Cemetery), is Vedado. This was and remains a wealthy area and its stately homes, some like small palaces, were built during the Belle Epoque. The tree-lined streets are quiet, a world away from Habana Vieja. La Rampa (the northern part of Calle 23, Malecón side) is Vedado's noisy, busy thoroughfare. After the 1950s it became a showcase for the city's modernity, where even a few skyscrapers grew, including the emblematic Hilton hotel, which during the revolution became the Hotel Tryp Habana Libre. Airline offices, travel agencies, banks, nightclubs and tourist restaurants abound in this district marked by architecture of the 1960s and 70s.

▶ **Access:** Vedado is pleasantly walkable but is much larger than Habana Vieja. The easiest way to cover ground is via taxi or **coco-taxi**.

▶ **Tips:** Orientation is simplified by the **street numbering system** indicated on posts at each intersection. The streets running southwest to northeast have **odd numbers** that increase from the Malecón to Plaza de la Revolución. The perpendicular streets are designated by letters A to P from east of Paseo to the seaside, and then by **even numbers** to the Almendares River. When walking through commercial areas you're likely to hear a "pssst" sound from people trying to get your attention (restaurant owners, cigar vendors, drivers, etc.). Just say no politely but firmly and continue walking.

AROUND LA RAMPA (CALLE 23)★

Map IV-A2

One of the busiest arteries in the city, Calle 23 runs through Vedado for more than 2km, from the Malecón to Colón Cemetery. The portion that climbs from the Hotel Nacional to Hotel Tryp Habana Libre is known as La Rampa. The frenetic activity of the day gives way only to the bars and discos of the many hotels.

The entrance to La Rampa is marked by the imposing silhouette of the **Hotel Nacional★** *(see Where to stay, p.78)*, a true emblem of the city: the building, crowned by two turrets, is unmistakable on its promontory at the foot of the Malecón. Since it opened in 1930, celebrities and dignitaries alike have descended on this luxurious Art Deco style establishment. Feel free to enter, especially to admire the **view★** of Havana Bay from the lovely garden. Below and to the west, at the corner of Malecón and Avenida 19, stand the two columns of the **monument to the Victims of Maine**. The memorial recalls the explosion of the battleship that marked the entry of the United States into the war against the Spanish on 15 February 1898. The remains of the ship are kept near this monument, which bears the names of the victims. This work, erected in 1925 to celebrate the friendship between Cubans and Americans, was partially destroyed by a cyclone the following year. In the aftermath

of the revolution, the bronze eagle that stood atop the monument and the busts of the American presidents were removed to protest the United States' policy against Cuba.

Note the **Edificio Focsa**, the highest skyscraper in the capital. This square-shaped building, at the corner of Calles 17 and M, has a bar-restaurant on the top floor, offering a sweeping **view★** of Havana.

The building that best symbolizes La Rampa remains the **Hotel Tryp Habana Libre,** formerly the Hilton. Completed in April 1957, this remnant of the American presence, nationalized after the revolution, is an excellent landmark when traveling in Vedado.

On the opposite side, at the corner of Calle L, a circular building, almost spaceship-like and typical of the 1960s, is nestled in the center of a pleasant square. The ice cream shop **Coppelia★** is a real institution immortalized by Tomás Gutiérrez Alea and Juan Carlos Tabío's film **Fresa y Chocolate** *(see next page)*. The choice of flavors here is often limited to vanilla and a few others, but Habaneros don't hesitate to wait an hour to enjoy one of these ice creams.

A few blocks away, at Avenida 17 502, between D and E, is the **Museo Nacional de Artes Decorativas★ (Map IV-A2)** (*☎7 830-9848-Tues-Sat 11am-6pm, Sun 9:30am-12:30pm - 5 CUC*). The lounges of this beautiful private mansion were decorated by the Maison Jansen in Paris at the beginning of the 20C. They each

45

Strawberry and Chocolate

The film Fresa y Chocolate, directed by Tomás Gutiérrez Alea and Juan Carlos Tabío, was a resounding international success after its release in 1994. This story of friendship and tolerance between a gay artist and a young communist student who supported the regime was partly filmed in Centro Habana. The film lives on mainly at **La Guarida**, *which deserves a visit (418 Calle Concordía, between Gervasio and Escobar, p. 60). Hidden on the top floor of a Belle Epoque palace, half abandoned, the apartment that was the setting for the film has become a paladar full of character. Often, in the morning, the restaurant's large white tablecloths dry in the building's former VIP lounge, undulating in the wind amid the ghostly decor of Corinthian columns and decrepit moldings.*

illustrate a theme: English lounge, Neoclassical, Art Deco, East Asian. The 18C furniture is the work of French cabinetmakers such as Boudin, Chevalier and Simoneau. On display are pieces of silverware, as well as porcelain from Sèvres, France. The small garden on the side offers a relaxing and cool retreat.

▷ *Walk towards the Malecón via Avenida de los Presidentes to the corner of Línea.*

Inaugurated in 1998 for the 50th anniversary of the Cuban National Ballet, the **Museo de la Danza (Map IV-A1)** (✆ 7 831 2198 - Tues-Sat 11am-6:30pm - 2 CUC) tells the story of dance through photos, costumes and paintings. The private collection of the great dancer Alicia Alonso makes up the the main collection of the museum, which has since been enriched by numerous donations.

THE HEIGHTS OF VEDADO

▷ *To reach the university from La Rampa, take Calle L two blocks southeast from the Hotel Tryp Habana Libre to the corner of Avenida 27.*

The **Universidad de La Habana (Map IV-B2)** was moved from Habana Vieja to this small hill in 1902. At the bottom of the enormous staircase leading to the university buildings stands a monument to Julio Mella, the founder of the Federation of Students and the Communist Party of Cuba, who was murdered in 1929. Behind the Neoclassical facade of the building is a small garden with lush vegetation.

Within the university, the **Museo Antropológico Montané** (✆ 7 832 1321 - Mon-Fri 8am-5pm - free) is dedicated to pre-Columbian artifacts. Behind the university, at Calle San Miguel 1159, the **Museo Napoleónico★** (✆ 7 879-1412 - Tues-Sat. 9:30am-4:30pm - hours subject to change - 3 CUC) houses one of the largest collections in the world dedicated to the Emperor Napoleon. Julio Lobo, a Cuban millionaire who was passionate about Napoleon I, had this palace built in the Florentine style. Porcelain from Sèvres decorates the living rooms filled with Empire furniture. Among the engravings and canvases, linger on the second floor in front of Jean-Georges Vibert's painting of Bonaparte preparing for his coronation ceremony. Many volumes on the life of Napoleon I and his era fill the library shelves. To the south of the university, on the other side of Avenida de los Presidentes, many health care facilities surround a hill. Cross the Ortopedico Hospital to access **Castillo del Príncipe**, a fortress built in 1779 to guard the surrounding area and prevent invasion attempts. This former prison is now a military area closed to the public, but there is an expansive view of the city from the top of the hill.

PLAZA DE LA REVOLUCIÓN

Map IV-A2

This huge plaza of 4.5ha can hold up to a million people during major political or cultural events. Cubans no longer gather here with quite such fervor but do come en masse for holidays like May 1, Labor Day. Normally, military personnel ensure that no one lingers on the square because of the many government buildings that surround it. The only photos allowed are those of the José Martí Memorial or the giant portrait of Che Guevara.

Begun in the 1950s under Batista, the Plaza de la Revolución was only completed after Castro came to power. In the center is a gigantic statue, the **José Martí memorial** *(enter the tower Mon-Sat 9am-5:30pm - 3 CUC),* a 142m-high obelisk in the shape of a five-pointed star. On the ground floor of the memorial, a few rooms are dedicated to the life and work of the "Apostle of Cuban Independence". The exhibition uses photos and personal objects supplemented by audio and video. From the top of the obelisk *(additional 2 CUC),* you can see the concrete buildings that surround the square and all of Havana. The glass walls are not ideal for taking photographs but the view is still lovely.

To the north, the facade of the Ministry of the Interior (Minint) is decorated with a **portrait of Che Guevara**, a huge black metal sculpture, next to a portrait of another important revolutionary figure, **Camilo Cienfuegos.**

To the right of Minint is the Ministry of Communications, housing the **Cuban Postal Museum** *(☎7-870-1551 - Mon-Fri 9am-5pm - free).* You can see a collection of stamps from all over the world here, sadly ironic in this country where the postal service leaves much to be desired.

To the east, the National Library faces the **Teatro Nacional** to the west.

To the south of the square, the offices of Líder Máximo occupy the **Grand Palacio de la Revolución**, the headquarters of the Central Committee of the Communist Party.

CEMENTERIO DE CRISTÓBAL COLÓN ★

Map IV-A3

Main entrance at the corner of Calles 12 and 25 - 8am-5pm - 5 CUC.
Located west of Plaza de la Revolución is this vast cemetery, surrounded by pale yellow walls. Enter through an immense Romanesque **portico** designed by Calixto de Loira in 1870. All architectural styles can be found here, where somber gray tombs stand next to richly ornate monuments. Some of Cuba's most prominent political and cultural personalities are interred in this cemetery (Fidel Castro is not among them, buried instead in Santa Ifigenia Cemetery in Santiago de Cuba).

The city of the dead is laid out in perfect grid formation, and the Neo-Byzantine central chapel serves as a good reference point for getting your bearings. The chapel's 19C **fresco** is the work of Cuban painter Miguel Melero.

Noteworthy monuments include the hard-to-miss **Monumento a los Bomberos** (main pathway), a huge sculpture dedicated to the 28 firemen who lost their lives in the fire of 17 May 1890.

The monument features the figures of the Angel of Death, torch in hand, and of a nun with a pelican at her feet.

The tomb of Doña Amelia de Gloria Castellano Pérez, nicknamed **La Milagrosa** (The Miraculous One), is a popular point of pilgrimage. As the story goes, when the tomb was opened the skeleton of Doña Amelia's child was found in her arms, although upon burial the child had been laid at its mother's feet. Since this discovery, pilgrims have visited the spot, leaving flowers and praying for Doña Amelia's aid.

The tomb of composer **Hubert de Blanck** bears a domino with double threes, evoking the game de Blanck was playing when he died.

The tomb of Cuban novelist **Alejo Carpentier** is here as well as that of 19C author **Cirilo Villaverde**, which lies not far from the resting place of

Cementerio de Cristóbal Colón

CEMENTERIO DE CRISTÓBAL COLÓN

0   100   200 m

Portada Principal

GENERAL MÁXIMO GÓMEZ BÁEZ

Alejo Carpentier

GALERÍA DE TOBÍAS

ESCULTURA DE RITA LONGA

Plaza N.O.

RÉPLICA DE LA OBRA LA PIEDAD DE MIGUEL ÁNGEL

Plaza Cristóbal Colón

Plaza N.E.

CARLOS J. FINLAY BARRES

ESTUDIANTES DE MEDICINA

Monumento a los Bomberos

La Milagrosa

Hubert de Blanck

FALLA-BONET

Cirilo Villaverde

Cecilia Valdés

PUERTA OESTE

Fray   Jacinto

VETERANOS DE LAS GUERRAS DE INDEPENDENCIA

Capilla central

Ave.   Obispo

PUERTA ESTE

COLONIA FRANCESA DE CUBA

MÁRTIRES DEL ASALTO AL PALACIO PRESIDENCIAL

PANTEÓN DE LAS FUERZAS ARMADAS REVOLUCIÓNARIAS

San Antonio Chiquito   PUERTA SUR

Ave. de Colón

N

Cecilia Valdés, the mulatta heroine of Villaverde's most famous novel of the same name, *Cecilia Valdés* (1882). Other highlights include the **angel doors** of the Catalina-Lasa Baró Art Deco mausoleum; the Art Deco Rita Longa **sculpture** inside the Aguilera tomb; and the **gold mural** by René Portocarrero inside the tomb of the Familía Raúl de Zárraga at Avenida Obispo Fray Jacinto and Calle 5.

Avenida Primera – This oceanfront avenue is not quite as pleasant and picturesque as the Malecón, but in summer, many of Havana's families find relief from the smothering heat at a little beach called Playita de 16 (between Calles 12 and 16), though Havana's inviting eastern beaches it's not (*see Playas del Este, p. 51*).

Miramar★

Miramar begins west of Vedado, beyond the mouth of the Río Almendares. It's a fashionable residential area with upscale hotels and restaurants that cater to a well-heeled clientele. Its wide, tree-lined avenues are flanked by stately mansions, many of them home to government offices, foreign corporations and most of Havana's embassies and consulates. The crumbling sidewalks and decaying villas that have seen better days, but this is still a pleasant neighborhood for strolling. Four long, busy thoroughfares run parallel to the ocean, beginning with Avenida 1 next to the coast, then Avenidas 3, 5, and 7.

▶ **Access:** Like Vedado, some areas of Miramar are walkable, but for longer distances take a taxi or coco-taxi.

▶ **Tip:** Odd-numbered avenues run east to west, crossing even-numbered streets.

If you need to buy clothing or groceries, Miramar has well-stocked **diplomercados.** These stores are no longer reserved solely for tourists or diplomats, but the items, sold at prohibitively high prices, are far from being within reach of many Cubans. The Cuban elite is particularly fond of **La Maison**, at the corner of Avenida 7 and Calle 16. In the lounges of this beautiful private mansion, you can buy perfumes, jewelery and clothing, though prices are likely higher than what you'd pay at home. Southeast of Miramar, across the woods of the charming **Kohly district** by Avenida 49-C, a small hilly road parallel to the Almendares River. Far from the city's bustle, crossing the park **Bosque de La Habana** provides a soothing feeling. The sound of footsteps is muffled by a carpet of foliage, the sunlight filterd through curtains of vines.

QUINTA AVENIDA★

Most embassies are concentrated around 5ta Avenida (no bikes allowed), one of the most beautiful arteries in Havana. Stone benches are set on a central path planted with laurel balls and palm trees. Between Calles 24 and 26, in Emiliano Zapata Park, is a handsome little rotunda with Corinthian columns and impressive scrollwork.

At the intersection of Calle 14, the **Museo del Ministerio del Interior** (☏7 202 1240 - Tues-Fri 9am-5pm, Sat 9am-2pm - 2 CUC) documents all of the United States' actions against Cuba. The CIA's methods of espionage are explained, as well as the failed attacks against Fidel Castro.

At the beginning of your trip, to get to know the city, visit the **Maqueta de la Habana (Map V-B1)**, (Calle 28 between Avenidas 1ra and 3ra - ☏7 202 7322). A gigantic, meticulous scale model of Havana (22mx10m), shows in impressive detail most of the

LA HABANA
MIRAMAR AND PLAYA
map V

0 — 1 km

NIGHTLIFE
Casa de la Musíca .... 🔟
Fábrica de Arte Cubano ... 1️⃣1️⃣
Tropicana .... 1️⃣2️⃣

GOLFO
DE MÉXICO

Acuario
Nacional
de Cuba 3️⃣4️⃣

Russian
Embassy

MIRAMAR

PARQUE
ECOLÓGICO
MONTE
BARRETO

PLAYA

QUEREJETA

BUENAVISTA

AEROPUERTO
MILITAR

Tropicana 1️⃣2️⃣

CIUDAD
ESCOLAR
LIBERTAD

WHERE TO STAY
Candy Mederos y
Alejandro .... 3️⃣4️⃣
Hotel Meliá Habana .... 3️⃣5️⃣

Teatro
Karl Marx
Playita del 16
Primera
Memorial de
Denuncia

Maqueta de
La Habana

Avenida

Quinta

Parque
Emiliano
Zapata

VEDADO

La Maison

LA HABANA VIEJA

KOHLY

Bosque
de La
Habana

SHOPPING
Galería La Acacia .... 1️⃣3️⃣

WHERE TO DRINK
El Cocinero .... 8️⃣
Habana Cafe .... 9️⃣

WHERE TO EAT
Aljibe (El) .... 2️⃣8️⃣
Cocina de Lilliam (La) .... 2️⃣9️⃣
Fuumiyaki .... 3️⃣0️⃣
Otramanera .... 3️⃣1️⃣
Palio (El) .... 3️⃣2️⃣

SANTA FÉ, MARINA HEMINGWAY

AUTOPISTA, PINAR DEL RIO

city's streets and buildings.
The striking constructivist-style
concrete tower that can be seen in
the distance is the **Russian embassy**,
located between Calles 62 and 66.
👥 A block before the Russian
Embassy, at the corner of Calle 60
and Avenida 1ra, is the **aquarium
(Map V-A1)** (📞 *[7] 202 5871 - www.*

*acuarionacional.cu - Tues-Sun
10am-6pm - 10 CUC, kids 7 CUC).* If
you've got kids in tow, this is an ideal
place to spend a couple of hours
seeing different sea creatures.

➲ *Grab a taxi along Avenida 5ta in the
direction of the port of Mariel until you
reach the Jaimanitas district.*

FUSTERLANDIA

Off map 👥 *Corner of Calle 226 and Ave. 3ra-A, Jaimanitas - 🕿 (7) 271 29 32. Fuster's studio is generally open daily 9am-4pm but it's possible neither he nor an assistant will be there. Free; donations welcome.*

Welcome to the enchanted world of José Fuster. His house and entire neighborhood are covered with multicolored mosaics, like something straight out of a fairy tale. Think Gaudí meets Picasso and Cheval. Fuster's work now spans more than 80 houses and has become delightful community project Fursterlandia.

FARTHER AFIELD

CASTILLO DE LOS TRES REYES DEL MORRO★

9am-8pm (times subject to seasonal variations) - 6 CUC and 2 CUC for the lighthouse, parking 1 CUC.

A huge chain blocking the entrance to the port once linked the fortress of San Salvador de la Punta to this castle, built between 1589 and 1630. Don't miss the 1844 **lighthouse**, from which the **view★★** of Havana is exceptional. **Los Doce Apóstoles** (The Twelve Apostles), the name given to the restaurant nestled within the walls, refers to the number of cannons intended to protect the city. Despite this protection system, Havana fell into the hands of the English in 1762. When King Carlos III recovered possession the following year, he ordered the construction of the Cabaña, a new fortress to the south of this site.

FORTALEZA DE SAN CARLOS DE LA CABAÑA

10am-10pm - 6 CUC before 6pm, 8 CUC after.

Completed in 1774, this fortress is one of the largest in Latin America. Following the triumph of the revolution, Che Guevara set up his HQ in this building, which was transformed into a military prison under the Republic. In the **Museo de la Comandancia de Che Guevara**, the journey of the famous guerrilla is traced through of photos, documents and personal effects. Also in the fortress is the **Parque Histórico Militar Morro-Cabaña**, which traces the military history of Cuba since its colonization through a collection of weapons. An interesting model shows the different stages of Havana's urbanization. Nightly from 8:30pm is a cannon ceremony with costumes from the Spanish colonial period.

PLAYAS DEL ESTE★

Half an hour's drive from Havana is this 24km strip of pretty white-sand beaches. Hire lounge chair and umbrellas (2 CUC each), snag coconuts from the roving vendors, and dine on just-caught seafood. To get there, take a colectivo (shared taxi) from right outside the main train station to Playa Santa Maria (expect to pay 2 CUC). There's also the T3 bus running every 40 min (9am-6pm) from Parque Central to Hotel Tropicoco (5 CUC). Or, ask your casa particular or hotel to arrange a taxi. 🚕 Expect to pay 50 CUC return.

Havana viewed from Castillo de los Tres Reyes del Morro

Addresses

Fábrica de Arte Cubano
© Soularue/hemis.fr

🍴
Where to eat

♿ *Find the addresses on our map using the numbers in the listing (e.g. ①). The coordinates in red (e.g. D2) refer to the detachable map inside the cover.*

HABANA VIEJA

See maps II (p. 16-17) and III (p. 22) and detachable map (inside cover).

Budget

③ Casa de la Para – *Map II-A3* - *Corner of Brasil and Bernaza* - ☎ *(7) 861 1626* - *11am-11pm* - *8/10 CUC*. This simple little eatery, formerly called Hanoi, is three blocks from the Capitol. You can sit in the dining room with its Creole decor or in the inner courtyard, shaded by a large *parra* (vine arbor). Stop in for salad, risotto, burger or fish of the day. Occasional jazz performance.

⑱ La Moneda Cubana – *Map II-A2* - *Calle San Ignacio 77 btwn Plaza de la Catedral and O'Reilly* - ☎ *(7) 867 3852* - *12:30pm-10pm* - *8/10 CUC*. Not far from Plaza de la Catedral, this tiny restaurant is perfect for a quick bite. Omelets, pork chops, black beans and rice and other Cuban specialties are available at low prices. The room is lined with coins and banknotes from all over the world; the collection is the pride of the owner.

Mid-range

① Al Carbón – *Map II-A2-B2* - *Calle Aguacate 9 at Chacon* - ☎ *(7) 863 9697* - *noon-midnight* - *15/20 CUC*. A friendly restaurant located a stone's throw from the Museum of the Revolution. The specialty here is grilled meats. Good atmosphere, warm welcome, and efficient service.

⑥ La Marina – *Map II-C3* - *Corner of Calles Brasil (Teniente Rey) and Oficios* - *12pm-11pm* - *10/15 CUC*. The large, open-air patio is bright and pleasant. The color blue dominates and, although the restaurant is in the heart of the city, there's a marina-like atmosphere. Fish is the star of the menu (grilled, skewered, etc.). Drink a glass of *guarapo*, fresh sugar cane juice made from the old school grinding machine in the corner.

⑨ O'Reilly 304 – *Map II-B2* - *Calle O'Reilly 304 btwn Habana and Aguiar* - ☎ *(7) 863 0206* - *11:45am-12am* - *15/20 CUC*. With a large Louise Bourgeois poster, a counter that doubles as seating, and cheerful and relaxed service, this kind of coffee shop would be the norm elsewhere; in Havana, it's a revolution. The young chefs know how to create well-balanced dishes, such as nicely grilled vegetables with a rather spicy fish, or a tangy lemon pie for dessert. Nice tapas and cocktail menu. Well worth a visit.

La Guarida

🔟 **Santo Ángel** – *Map II-C3* - *Plaza Vieja (corner Brasil and San Ignacio) - ✆ (7) 861 1626 - noon-midnight - 15/25 CUC.* In a coveted location on Plaza Vieja, in the shade of a noble colonnade. The setting is rather chic, but the price-quality ratio is also favorable. To eat, gazpacho, beef with wine sauce and, for once, a rather full dessert menu (lemon pie, cheesecake, etc.). Drinks are more expensive. Service can be slow.

⓫ **La Taberna del Pescador** – *Map II-B3* - *Calle San Ignacio 260A btwn Amargura and Lamparilla - ✆ 53 34 3537 (mobile) - noon-midnight - 10/15 CUC.* There are just a handful of wooden tables at this tiny restaurant where fish all over the walls announce that the sea dictates the menu. Fish soup, octopus, shrimp enchilado, grilled lobster, and their ilk are all fresh and tasty.

⓮ **La Dominica** – *Map III-A2* - *O'Reilly 108 at Mercaderes - ✆ (7) 860 2918 - noon-midnight - 12/25 CUC.* A pleasant place to break for lunch is this restaurant's large terrace. It's charming, especially in the evening, under the stars and with the help of good Cuban musicians. The menu is 100% Italian: low-cost pasta and pizzas, or more elaborate specialties (*vitello alla romana*).

⓯ **Doña Eutimia** – *Map III-A1* - *Callejón del Chorro 60C, just off San Ignacio, btwn Empedrado and O'Reilly - ✆ (7) 861 1332 - 10am-9:30pm- 15/20 CUC.* On a pretty street overlooking Plaza de la Catedral, this popular paladar— slightly a victim of its own success—requires you to book well in advance! The cuisine is not off the beaten track (fried and grilled meats and seafood, *arroz moro* aka rice and beans), etc., but each dish is particularly well done. The beautiful terrace and retro decor are an added draw.

⓰ **Este No Es Un Cafe** – *Map III-A1* - *Callejón del Chorro 58A, just off San Ignacio, btwn Empedrado and O'Reilly - ✆ (7) 862 5109 - www. estonoesuncafe.com - noon-midnight - 15/20 CUC.* "This is not a café," says the sign, and indeed this is part art gallery (look upstairs), part modern restaurant. The tiny room on the ground floor overflows into the alleyway where a few tables are arranged. It's a pleasant setting, with the Plaza de la Catedral in sight. Munch on grilled chicken with sautéed vegetables, fish of the day, etc.

Treat Yourself

② **Café del Oriente** – *Map II-C3* - *Plaza San Francisco de Asís (corner of Oficios and Amargura) - ✆ (7) 860 6686 - 11am-midnight - 25/50 CUC.* High columns, white tablecloths, well-dressed waiters, and a pianist make this one of the chicest restaurants in Havana. Continental fare is served here, with good use of fresh seafood. Prices are high for à la carte, but the quality is there.

⑦ **Los Mercaderes** – *Map II-C3* - 1/F, *Calle Mercaderes 207 btwn Lamparilla and Amargura - ✆ (7) 861 2437- noon-midnight - 25/35 CUC.* An

© Yoko Aziz/age fotostock

Walls of La Bodeguita del Medio

authentic paladar, set in a beautiful apartment, with a succession of rooms distinguished by high ceilings, beautiful ceramic tiles, and antique furniture and wall-hangings. Intimate atmosphere, even more so if you've got a table near the balcony overlooking the street. The chef creates original and meticulous Cuban cuisine, with a specialty lobster with coffee dish. Lunch menu at 20 CUC. Live music.

12 La Bodeguita del Medio – *Map III-A1* - Calle Empedrado 207 btwn Cuba and San Ignacio - ℘ (7) 867 1374 - 12pm-1am - 15/30 CUC. A stone's throw from Plaza de la Catedral is this, Havana's most famous tavern, slinging drinks and food since 1942.

Hemingway used to drink mojitos here after filling up on some daiquiris at Floridita. Its walls are covered in photos, graffiti and the signatures of clients. Quality Creole cuisine and a whole range of cocktails, including the famous mojito, to enjoy to music. Sit at the bar, in the dining room or on the pleasant terrace on the first floor. Reservations recommended.

17 Mama Inés – *Map III-B2* - Calle de la Obrapía 60 btwn Oficios and Baratillo - ℘ (7) 862 2669 - 20/25 CUC. Erasmo, once Fidel Castro's personal chef, is doing booming business in the private sector with this popular restaurant. He cooks carefully according to the fresh products he has managed to find: squid salad, grilled

© Claire Boobbyer/Michelin

San Cristóbal

meats, assorted fish... Everything is fresh, prepared with simplicity and precision, and respects regional flavors: really good news in Havana! A drink or two on the charming side terrace, where a singer sometimes performs, makes for a nice evening out (kitchen closes at 10pm).

Splurge

19 El Templete – *Map III-B1* - *Corner of Ave. del Puerto and Narciso López, ℘ (7) 866 88 07 - noon-midnight - around 30 CUC.* When it opened in 2004, this restaurant immediately became one of the best in the capital, thanks in particular to its menu of meticulously cooked fish. A dozen years later it remains quite popular, though it now has some competition.

CENTRO HABANA

Budget

20 3 Chinitos – *Map IV-C2* - *Calle Dragones 355-357 btwn Manrique and San Nicolás - ℘ (7) 863 3388 - noon-midnight - 5/15 CUC.* In the heart of Barrio Chino, this room transports guests to the Far East...a Cuban version. Cuban Chinese is greasy-delicious and you'll see this as soon as you walk in, tables full of happy guests. There's fried rice and chop suey, and some straight Cuban dishes like fried plantain. A meal here is a pleasant and unpretentious experience.

Treat Yourself

22 Casa Miglis – *Map IV-C1* - *Calle Lealtad 120 btwn Ánimas and Lagunas - ℘ (7) 864 1486 - www. casamiglis.com - noon-1am - around 25 CUC.* Not far from the Malecón is this pretty restaurant, with thoughtful decor (contemporary works of art on the walls, antique moldings and tiles). It was created by Michel Miglis, a Swede of Greek origin who fell in love with Cuba when he came to make a documentary. The menu is Northern Europe meets the Caribbean.

25 ☺ La Guarida – *Map IV-C2* - *2/F, Calle Concordía 418 btwn Gervasio and Escobar - ℘ (7) 866 9047 - www. laguarida.com - noon-midnight - 25/35 CUC.* At first sight, this small Belle Epoque palace looks abandoned. By taking the superb marble staircase, you'll discover on the first floor a large salon (moldings, columns, peeling paintings). The *paladar* is set above this, in a small apartment that's retained its original character, so it now seems retro. The place is worthy of a movie set, and indeed it's here that *Fresa y Chocolate* was partly shot *(see p. 46)*. The walls are covered with photos of the many celebrities who have since passed through to eat octopus carpaccio with pepper sauce; grilled chicken with honey and lemon; and, for dessert, the essential strawberry and chocolate! Reservation required for dinner.

㉗ San Cristóbal – *Map IV-C2* - *Calle San Rafael 469 btwn Lealtad and Campanario* - *☎ (7) 867 9109* - *www. paladarsancristobal.com* - *every day but Sunday noon-midnight* - *15/30 CUC*. This pretty residence seems frozen in time: along a patio, are small rooms full of character, all woodwork, old photos and religious objects. The cuisine reflects Cuban tradition; the ingredients are fresh and the servings generous.

VEDADO

Mid-range

㉓ La Casona de 17 – *Map IV-B1* - *Ave. 17 60 btwn M and N* - *☎ (7) 838 3136* - *8am-11:30pm* - *15/20 CUC*. Opposite the Edificio Focsa is this restaurant in an old house serving standard Cuban cuisine (chicken fricassee, pork cutlet, etc.). The restaurant is part dining room, part more casual (and less expensive) *parillada* (grill). This food is not

mind-blowing but is tasty and well-priced for the neighborhood. Service is slow; don't come here if you're in a rush.

㉖ La Rampa – *Map IV-B1* - *Corner of 23 and L (ground floor of Hotel Tryp Habana Libre)* - *24/7* - *10/15 CUC*. On La Rampa (part of Avenida 23), this large cafeteria evokes an American diner of the 1950s: no coincidence, it's located in the former Hilton, built in 1958. This is one of the few places where, at a reasonable price and in air conditioning, you can eat sandwiches, pasta and pizza.

㉛ Fuumiyaki – *Map V-B1* - *Ave. 26 367 btwn 23 and 25* - *☎ (7) 8337939* - *noon-midnight* - *10/12 CUC*. Even a few years ago it was unimaginable that this proper Japanese restaurant, with its streamlined red and black decor, would open in Havana. Judging by the full tables, Fuumiyaki is thriving, and with good reason: its chefs consistently turn out delicious sushi (nigiri and maki), yakitori, soba, and tempura.

Treat Yourself

㉑ Café Laurent – *Map IV-B1* - *Calle M 257 btwn 19 and 21 (top floor, access by elevator)* - *☎ (7) 832 6890* - *noon-midnight* - *15/30 CUC*. As lively and noisy as La Rampa district is, this airy white paladar hidden on the top of a small apartment building is a haven of peace and tranquility. Gauzy white fabric floats in the breeze. Snag a seat on the large, shaded terrace and dig into a fair number of vegetarian options, as well as nicely cooked meats and seafood. Reservations recommended.

MIRAMAR AND MARIANAO

Mid-range

31 Otramanera – *Map V-B1* - *Avenida 35 1018 btwn 18 and 20* - ☏ (7) 203 8315 - otramaneralahabana.com/en - 12:30pm-11pm closed Sun and Mon - 15/25 CUC. A pair of Catalans are doing remarkable things here, a favorite of young and trendy Habaneros who grab outdoor tables and seats at the bar. To eat, nicely presented fish of the day, sardines with grilled eggplant and pumpkin, skewers of marinated beef served with fried yucca. A lively vibe, well done cocktails and a small dessert list, including delicious rice pudding, make this a worthy stop.

32 El Palio – *Map V-B1* - *1ra 2402 corner of 24* - ☏ (7) 202 9867 - noon-midnight - 15/25 CUC. A stone's throw from the sea is this *paladar* whose name refers to the famous horse race in Siena, Italy; you'll see photos to match on the walls. The food, however, skews Cuban, with lots of fresh seafood.

28 El Aljibe – *Map V-B1* - *Ave. 7ma btwn 24 and 26* - ☏ (7) 204 4233 - 12pm-11:30pm - 15/25 CUC. This huge thatched-roof hut has been hosting groups big and small for more than 60 years, but the quality has miraculously not gone downhill. Chicken plays a starring role here, with a specialty of pollo criollo (Creole-style), accompanied by rice, salad, potatoes

and plantains fried to order. Good wine cellar.

Mid-range

29 La Cocina de Lilliam – *Map V-B1* - *Calle 48 1311, btwn 13 and 15* - ☏ (7) 209 6514 - www.lacocinadelilliam.com - noon-midnight - 20/50 CUC. This *paladar* is proud of former US president Jimmy Carter, who ate there in 2002, 21 years after the end of his presidency. Sumptuous house, superb garden with fountains and greenery, and delicious standard Cuban fare elevated with top ingredients and execution. The only thing lacking a bit is the service, which can be disorganized. Plan for a leisurely evening.

WHERE TO SNACK

☺ **Good to know** – Some hotels serve drinks in chic environs and at reasonable prices. Hotels Ambos Mundos or Saratoga have beautiful roof terraces, while Hotel Nacional, with its superb garden overlooking the sea and the city, is a must.

Cafes

4 El Escorial – *Map II-C3* - *Plaza Vieja, Calle Mercaderes 317 at Muralla (Habana Vieja)* - ☏ (7) 868 3545 - 9am-11pm. On Plaza Vieja you can find excellent coffee, roasted and ground on the spot. Come before 9am if you want to avoid the lines. The *grano arábico* comes from the Sierra del Escambray region, north of Trinidad. On the terrace, which faces the square, sit with a cup and munch on sandwiches or pastries.

© phelder2006/iStockphoto.com

Coppelia

13 Café O'Reilly – *Map III-A2* - *Calle O'Reilly 203 btwn San Ignacio and Cuba (Habana Vieja) - ☎ (7) 863 6684 - 9am-midnight.* Huge sacks of coffee from Pinar del Río province await roasting and grinding on site at this trendy café. Snag a seat for a *café cubano* and people watching. Sandwiches also served.

Hot Chocolate

8 Museo del Chocolate – *Map II-C3* - *Calle Mercaderes 255 btwn Amargura and Brasil (Habana Vieja) - ☎ (7) 866 4431 - 11am-7:30pm.* This is mecca for chocolate addicts. Sit down and order a hot chocolate (approx. 0.60 CUC) or cold chocolate (approx. 1 CUC). Both are a delight! A small collection of antique and vintage chocolate-production equipment lends this cafe its name. You can also buy chocolate in all shapes (frogs, horses, houses, and so on.).

Ice Cream

21 Coppelia – *Map IV-B1* - *Corner of La Rampa and L (Vedado) - ☎ (7) 832 6184 - 11am-9pm.* On architecture alone, this Cuban Revolution modernist ice cream parlor is a hit. That it was featured in beloved film *Fresa y Chocolate* has made it quite popular. Habaneros can queue for hours for a cone. Be aware that the sales kiosk located on La Rampa side is reserved for tourists; payment is in CUC and the lines are shorter. There are few flavors on offer, usually just chocolate, vanilla, and sometimes strawberry.

5 Helad'oro – *Map II-B2* - *Calle Aguíar 208 btwn Empredrado and Tejadillo - ☎ 53 05 9131 (mobile) - noon-10pm (11pm Fri-Sun).* An excellent ice-cream parlor for a break when visiting Old Havana. There are flavors here for all taste buds!

Where to drink

🍹 **Find the addresses on our maps using the numbers in the listing (e.g. ❶). The coordinates in red (e.g. D2) refer to the detachable map (inside cover).**

HABANA VIEJA

❶ **El Almedron** – *Map II-C3* - *Plaza Vieja, corner of Muralla and San Ignacio* - 📞 *(5) 255 8716 - www. facebook.com/elAlmendronCuba* - *noon-midnight Sun-Thurs, Fri-Sat 3am.* Beautiful stained glass marks the entrance to this café that boasts one thing nowhere else in Havana has:

free wifi. That alone is reason enough to come here and linger over coffee, a cocktail, or a cold Cristal beer. The bar is built of car tires and, on the walls, hang photos and drawings of the vintage cars that cruise around the city.

❷ **Cerveceria Factoria Plaza Vieja** – *Map II-C3* - *Plaza Vieja, corner of Muralla and San Ignacio* - 📞 *(7) 866 4453 -noon-midnight.* Right on Plaza Vieja is this brewery, serving its beer by the meter (literally) on its large terrace. Small menu of snacks. Very popular for people-watching.

❸ **El Floridita** – *Map II-A3* - *Corner of Calle Obispo and Ave. de Bélgica* - 📞 *(7) 867 1300 - www. elfloridita.net - 11am-midnight.* A real institution founded in 1817 and famous for its daiquiri, a favorite of loyal customer Ernest Hemingway. Expect to pay 6-8CUC for a cocktail. Chic and touristy atmosphere.

❹ **La Bodeguita del Medio** – *Map III-A1* - *See "Where to Eat" (Habana Vieja).* A must to enjoy a mojito in the footsteps of Ernest Hemingway. The atmosphere is always lively: you have to make your way through a packed crowd, including musicians, to place an order. Expect to pay 8-10CUC for a cocktail.

CENTRO HABANA

❺ **Bembe** – *Map IV-C2* - *corner Amistad and Barcelona* - 📞 *(7)*

Cerveceria Factoria Plaza Vieja

© ToniFlap/iStockphoto.com

© Malecón 663

Malecón 663

8666 288 - www.facebook.com/ BembeTapasBar. Half a block from El Capitolio, its entrance marked by handsome scrollwork, is this welcoming little pub with daily happy hour. Sip a cold Cristal beer or a piña colada or mojito brimming with fresh mint. To eat are empanadas, guacamole and chips, fried plantains, grilled shrimp, and other small bites.

VEDADO

6 **Encuentro** – *Map IV-A1* - *Linea 112 btwn M and L* - *ℰ (7) 8329 744* - *www.facebook.com/ Encuentro-329944737150384*. This popular rooftop bar starts filling up only in the wee hours after midnight, though if you come before then you can enjoy a low-key drink. Most popular here are rum-based cocktails.

Though Cuban music plays from the stereo and you'll see some tables smoking hookah, this is not a loud, bumping club.

7 **Malecón 663** – *Map IV-C1* - Malecón 663 btwn Belascoain and Gervasio - *ℰ (7) 8601 459* - *www. malecon663.com/es/home*. On the roof of a charming *casa particular* hides a bar with a sweeping view of the Malecón, ideal for sunset drinks. Sip cocktails (daquiri, mojito)or take a glass of sangria.

8 **El Cocinero** – *Map V-B1* - *Calle 26 btwn 11 and 13, right next to La Fabrica* - *ℰ (7) 832355* - *www. elcocinerocuba.com/esr*. In a former peanut oil factory is this restaurant and rooftop bar. Sit for a full meal, or munch on a sandwich as you sip a mango mojito on the shaded roof terrace.

🛍 *Shopping*

🔊 ind the addresses on our maps using the numbers in the listing (e.g. (e.g. ❶). The coordinates in red (e.g. D2) refer to the detachable map (inside cover).

Markets

❿ **Agromercado Vedado** – *Map IV-A2* - Calle B btwn 17 and 19 (Vedado). Fruits, vegetables and lots of local flavor.

Mercado de Libros – *Map III-B2* - Plaza de Armas, O'Reilly at Oficios (Habana Vieja) - Daily except Sun. Expect to find plenty of books by Fidel Castro, Che Guevara, Fernando Ortiz and Nicolás Guillén along with others, sometimes in English. Relatively high posted prices, but bargaining is possible. Vendors sometimes have a handful of antique or vintage goods.

Mall

⓬ **Plaza Carlos III** – *Map IV-B2* - Ave. Salvador Allende (Carlos III) btwn Retiro and Arbol Seco (Centro Habana) - 9am-7pm. If you're in Havana and you need to buy shoes or clothing, this popular mall is your best bet. Weekends see the food court full of families.

Rum

❸ **Casa del Ron** – *Map II-A3* - Baratillo 53 at Obispo (Habana Vieja) - ☎ (7) 866 8476 - Mon-Thurs 9am-5:30, Fri-Sun 9am-4:30pm. In a corner of Plaza de Armas is the House of Rum.

Tasting and sale of many rum brands, as well as cigars. You can also buy rum at **Museo del Ron** (See p. 46).

Cigars

❷ **La Casa del Habano** – *Map II-C3* - Corner of Mercaderes and Lamparilla (inside Conde Villanueva hotel, Habana Vieja) - ☎ (7) 862 92 93 - lacasadelhabano.com - 11am-7pm. A humble independent cigar joint this is not. Casa del Habano is a big franchise, with branches as far flung as Armenia, Gibraltar, and Australia (plus a handful across Cuba). Solid selection of the best Cuban cigars (Robaina, Montecristo, Cohiba, etc.).

❼ **Partagás** – *Map II-A3* - Calle Industria 520 btwn Dragones and Barcelone (just behind the Capitol, Centro Habana) - ☎ (7) 866 8060 - 9am-7pm (Sun 2pm). A very wide choice of cigars on the historic site of the (now relocated) oldest tobacco factory in the city (see p. 42).

Handicrafts

❶ **Almacenes San José** – *Map II-C4* - Calle Desamparados at Cuba (Habana Vieja) - 9:30am-6:30pm. On the docks south of Habana Vieja, this former maritime warehouse has been converted into a huge craft market. The aisles are lined in hundreds of stalls selling wooden sculptures, clothing, jewelery, hats, etc. Every imaginable souvenir is available. Note that some vendors can be a bit pushy.

Mercado de Libros, Plaza de Armas

🛍

Haggling is expected, but do not haggle for sport.

⑤ Palacio de la Artesanía –
Map II-B2 - *In Palacio Pedroso, Calle Cuba 64, btwn calles Peña Pobre and Tacón (Habana Vieja) - 9:30am-7pm.* This beautiful 18C residence was built for a former mayor of Havana. The patio and rooms on the first floor house many shops, mixing souvenirs and crafts: jewelery, clothing, the occasional CD, musical instruments, wooden statuettes, etc.

⑥ Souvenir stands are set up every day but Sun. on the **Parque Céspedes *(Map II-B2)*,** behind the cathedral and in Vedado, at the corner of **La Rampa** and **Calle M *(Map IV-B1)*.** On offer are palm hats, carved coconuts, Che T-shirts, and small figurines.

⑧ Soldadito de Plomo – *Map II-C3* - *Calle Muralla 164 btwn Plaza Vieja and Cuba (Habana Vieja) - ✆ (7) 866 0232 - Mon-Fri 9am-5pm, Sat 9am-1:30pm.* This shop, named and selling lead toy soldiers, stocks tiny lead versions of Che Guevara, José Martí and others.

Art galleries

④ Casa Oswaldo Guayasamín – *Map II-C2*- *Calle Obrapía 111 btwn Mercaderes and Oficios (Habana Vieja) - ✆ (7) 861 3843 - Tues-Sat 9:30-5pm, Sun 9:30am-5pm.* Ecuadorian artist Guayasamín, known in particular for his portrait of Fidel (visible on the first floor), has his Cuban studio here: sculptures, paintings, ceramics and jewelery, to be discovered among the works of other artists.

⑨ Taller Experimental de Gráfica – *Map III-A1* - *Callejón del Chorro 62, just off San Ignacio, btwn Empedrado and O'Reilly (Habana Vieja) - ✆ (7) 862 0979 - Mon-Fri 11am-5pm.* Just off Plaza de la Catedral, this large engraving workshop is in working order, as evidenced by the smell of ink. Browse the wide choice of prints, in all sizes and prices, signed by young Cuban artists. The artists are happy to chat about their work.

⑪ Galería Habana – *Map IV-A1* - *Calle Línea 460 btwn E and F (Vedado) - ✆ (7) 832 7101 - www.galerihabana.com - Mon-Fri 8:30am-5:30pm.* Since May 1962 this gallery has been showcasing the work of Cuban artists, some well-known (Wifredo Lam, Amelia Pelaez), others rising.

⑬ Galería La Acacia – *Map V-B1* - *Calle 18 512 btwn 5 and 7 (Miramar) - ✆ (7) 214 1444 - www.galerialacacia. com - Mon-Fri 9am-5pm, Sat 9am-1pm.* This prominent gallery, established in Miramar in 1981, promotes contemporary Cuban works.

Nightlife

*♪ **Find the addresses on our maps using the numbers in the listing (e.g. ①). The coordinates in red (e.g. D2) refer to the detachable map (inside cover).***

HABANA VIEJA

Live music and dancing

Music is everywhere in Havana. There are few meals in restaurants where you won't also enjoy a performance. It's nearly impossible to draw up an exhaustive list of places to go. See **www.lapapeleta.cult.cu** for daily cultural programming.

③ **Maragato** – *Map III-A2* - *Corner of Calles Obispo and Cuba, within Hotel Florida (See Where to stay p. 84)* - *℘ (7) 862 4127 - daily from 9pm - admission 6 CUC with a drink.* This intimate piano bar opens onto the patio of the beautiful Hotel Florida, one of the handful of places in Habana Vieja to dance salsa. The bar is mostly frequented by tourists but is pleasant.

VEDADO

⑤ **Café Cantante Mi Habana** – *Map IV-A3*- *Plaza de la Revolución (corner of Paseo and 39) - from 5pm and 9pm - approx. 10 CUC according to the schedule.* Under Teatro Nacional, this hall hosts the largest salsa groups. The place turns into a disco on evenings without a performance *(9pm-5am 10 CUC).* No shorts.

El Gran Palenque – *off map* - *Calle 4 103 corner of Calle 5 - ℘ (7) 833 4560 - www.folkcuba.cult.cu - Sat from 3pm- approx. 6 CUC.* When not touring the world, this folk dance group—founded in 1962 and famous for its traditional Afro-Cuban percussion and dance—performs a popular, frenzied Saturday rumba.

② **Gran Teatro de la Habana** – *Map II-A3* - *Paseo de Martí 458 btwn El Capitolio and Hotel Inglaterra - ℘ (7) 8613 077 - www.balletcuba.*

© Abel Ernesto/Michelin

Ballet Nacional de Cuba

cult.cu. The facade of this theater, built in 1838 and expanded in 1915, is sumptuous. Within performs the Cuban National Ballet—some of the world's top dancers.

⑨ **Teatro Nacional** – *Map IV-A3* - *Plaza de la Revolución (corner of Paseo and 39) - ℘ (7) 878 0771 - www. teatronacional.cu.* Often hosts troupes of actors from abroad, as well as the National Symphony Orchestra.

VEDADO

⑧ **Teatro Amadeo Roldán** – *Map IV-A1* - *Corner of Ave. 7ᵐᵃ and Calle D - ℘ 832 1168.* This large space, in a new-ish building rebuilt as it was in the 1920s, is one of the best places to listen to classical music concerts. Program displayed in the lobby.

① **Habana Café** – *Map I-C2* - *Inside hotel Meliá Cohiba, btwn 1ʳᵃ and 3ʳᵃ (Paseo) - ℘ (7) 833 3636 - daily from 9pm - 30 CUC w/drinks, 50 CUC w/ dinner.* Dotted with vintage cars, motorcycles, and airplanes is this throwback to the 1950s, with nightly live music. It's over the top and a little expensive, but where else can you dance next to a classic Chevy with gleaming tailfins?

CENTRO HABANA

⑦ **Casa de la Música** – *Map IV-C2* - *Calle Galiano 255 btwn Neptuno and Concordía - ℘ (7) 862 4165 - concerts 5pm-7pm (15 CUC) and 11pm-3am.* All types of Cuban music are well represented here. The biggest Havana groups will usually perform at the end of the week. Check who's playing before you go (ask your hotel or casa to call), because it's 15CUC cover whether it's a mediocre performer or a big show, and the quality varies significantly. There's also a branch in Miramar at *corner of Ave. 35 and Calle 20 - ℘ (7) 202 6147 - admission 15 CUC - concerts 5pm-9pm, 11pm-3am*

⑥ **Callejón de Hamel** – *Map IV-B2* - *Btwn Aramburu and Hospital, near San Lázaro.* This alleyway with its brightly painted walls is an open-air cultural center for exhibitions, street shows, and rumba concerts (Sunday from noon).

MIRAMAR

⑪ 🎧 **Fábrica de Arte Cubano** – *Map V-B1* - *Corner of 26 and 11 - www.fabricadeartecubano.com - Thurs-Sun 4pm-2am - admission 2 CUC.* In 2014 an abandoned warehouse space opened as Havana's hottest place to drink, eat, and dance. There are art exhibitions. There's live music. There's a tapas bar. On the roof locals and visitors from around the globe sip potent mojitos and mingle. You could be in New York, Berlin, or London, but you're in Havana! Live performances most nights, by mostly Cuban musicians playing to a packed house.

© Peter Schickert/imageBROKER/age fotostock

Tropicana

Clubs and cabaret

VEDADO

④ **Cabaret Parisién** – *Map IV-B1* - *In Hotel Nacional (See Where to stay) - ☎ (7) 836 35 64/67 - from 10pm - approx. 35 CUC.* The nightclub of Hotel Nacional offers quality shows and pumping Cuban dance and music Almost all tourists but a fun evening. We recommend skipping the food here.

MARIANAO

⑫ **Tropicana** – *Map V-B2* - *Corner of Calle 72 and Ave. 43 - ☎ (7) 267 0174 - www.cabaret-tropicana.com - daily from 10pm except Mon - 75/85/ 95 CUC.* Since 1939, this institution has welcomed the likes of Nat King Cole and Maurice Chevalier. Today, more than 200 dancers perform here. Lights, glitter and feathers are everywhere. Despite its sky-high price, the Tropicana is often full of tour groups, so book ahead.

Where to stay

Accommodations in Havana are either in hotels or in *casas particulares,* homey guesthouses that range from humble to grand.

♿ *Find the addresses on our maps using the numbers in the listing (e.g. ❶). The coordinates in red (e.g. D2) refer to the detachable map (inside cover).*

HABANA VIEJA

Budget

❶ **Casa Ana y Suráma** – *Map II-C3* - *2/F, Calle San Ignacio 454 btwn Sol and Santa Clara* - *♧ (7) 862 2717* - *www.anaysurama.blogspot.com* - ▦ ✕ - *3 rooms, 35 CUC.* In a 1925 building ideally located near Plaza Vieja, this apartment preserves the spirit of the Belle Epoque: Corinthian columns in the large living room, multiple stained glass windows, and statues, porcelains, and canvases throughout. The rooms have the same handsome decor, though note that only one has a private bathroom.

❹ **Casa Colonial Azul** – *Map II-C4* - *1/F, Calle San Ignacio 654 btwn Merced and Jesús María* - *♧ (7) 863 1279* - ▦ ✕ - *4 rooms, 30 CUC.* Right next to Greenhouse is the Blue House, in a handsome bright blue. Rooms are simple but comfortable, and the location very practical for sightseeing.

❺ **Colonial Habana Susi** – *Map II-B3* - *2/F, Calle Amargura 260 btwn Compostela and Habana* - *♧ (7) 861 7265* - ▦ ✕ - *6 rooms,*

30 CUC. It's impossible not to notice the pretty white and pistachio facade of this house. On the second floor, the apartment—renovated by Susi to preserve "the colonial style that appeals so much to tourists"—overflows with colors, including beautiful cement tiles covering the floors. From the roof terrace take in a breathtaking view of the Capitol.

❽ **Casa Cristo Colonial** – *Map II-B3* - *1/F, Calle Cristo 16 btwn Brasil and Muralla* - *♧ (7) 862 8779* - *www. casacristocolonial.com* - ▦ ✕ - *2 rooms, 38 CUC.* A large patio covered with *azulejos* (Portuguese painted tiles), high ceilings, and original 1920s elements, all lovingly tended to by Belkis and Jeiver, a young couple—with two children—who demonstrate that with a lot of energy and modest means, the renewal of Old Havana is possible.

❾ **Greenhouse** – *Map II-C4* - *1/F, Calle San Ignacio 656 btwn Merced and Jesús María* - *♧ (7) 862 9877* - *fabio.quintana@infomed.sld.cu* - ▦ ✕ - *7 rooms, 35 CUC.* This building's green facade makes it stand out. Brothers Fabio and Eugenio host a slew of nationalities, who take breakfast together in the dining room. Each room is decorated differently, but all have antique furniture, gold accents and bright colors.

❿ **Casa Humberto** – *Map II-B3* - *2/F, Calle Compostela 611 btwn Sol and Luz* - *♧ (7) 860 3264* - *www. casahumberto.com* - ▦ ✕ - *4 rooms,*

32 CUC. A pleasant, safe place where you can feel at ease. Humberto has lovingly preserved the character of his old house. Try to get the room on the roof terrace, which offers a superb view of the city!

12 Casa Jesús y María –
Map II-B3 - *Calle Aguacate 518 btwn Sol and Muralla* - 🖉 *(7) 861 13 78* -
🍽 ✕ - *6 rooms, 30 CUC.* A real retreat driven by an outstanding sense of hospitality and service. María and Jesús never cease to improve their little house, where every piece of decor—from the wooden flamingo to the porcelain dog—shows thought. The rooms nestled on the roof terrace, a real green oasis, are the most pleasant. It's up here that you can have breakfast.

15 Casa Nancy – **Map II-B3** - *1/F, Calle Brasil (Teniente Rey) 207 btwn Habana and Aguiar* - 🍽 ✕ - *3 rooms, 38 CUC.* Nancy was one of the pioneers of Havana's guest houses. The rooms here open onto a quiet patio filled with lush green plants. Comfortable, family atmosphere.

16 Casa Nelson – **Map II-C4** - *Calle Merced 14 btwn San Ignacio and Oficios* - 🖉 *(7) 860 3987* - 🍽 ✕ - *5 rooms, 30 CUC.* This is an authentic example of how, after the revolution, these old houses were divided up for several families: this house could win the prize for narrowness! The rooms open onto the thin courtyard, dark indeed but sheltered from the noises of the street. Simplicity and cleanliness are the order of the day,

all with a decor that could win a prize for kitsch!

25 Casa Marivelas – **Map III-A1** - *1/F, Calle Empedrado 211 btwn Cuba and San Ignacio* - 🖉 *(7) 640 0688* - 🍽 - *2 rooms, 50 CUC.* A stone's throw from the cathedral, at the end of a courtyard protected from the hustle and bustle of the street, are two studio apartments with a stocked kitchenette (a tasty breakfast is prepared by a neighbor). Apartment 25 is relatively simple; apartment 29 is more renovated.

Treat Yourself

3 Hostal Calle Habana – **Map II-B3** - *Calle Habana 559 btwn Brasil and Amargura* - 🖉 *(7) 867 4081* - *www. hostalcallehabana.com* - 🍽 ✕ - *6 rooms, 50/75 CUC.* In contrast to the street's more-than-decayed facades is this small pink house with handsome wooden shutters, a detail that indicates a quality renovation. This mid-range *casa particular*'s decor mixes concrete, wood and florals. Rooms are colorful, contemporary and neat. Nice, airy breakfast space.

7 Convento de Santa Brigida y Madre Isabel – **Map II-C3** - *Calle Calle Oficios 204 btwn Brasil and Muralla* - 🖉 *(7) 866 43 15* - 🍽 - *19 rooms, 50/75 CUC* 🛏. Praise be to the nuns who have transformed part of their magnificent convent—next to the church of San Francisco de Asis—into a well-maintained guesthouse. The rooms, cozy and perfectly equipped, offer peace in the heart of the old city.

Splurge

2 Hotel Beltrán de Santa Cruz –
Map II-C2 - *Calle San Ignacio 411 btwn
Muralla and Sol - ✆ (7) 860 8330 -
▤ - 12 rooms, 150/200 CUC ⬚.*
Well located a stone's throw from
the beautiful Plaza Vieja, this former
residence, once owned by a family
of Spanish notables, preserves its
colonial character around a pretty
green patio. The charm works despite
some rooms showing their age.

6 Conde de Villanueva –
Map II-C2 - *Corner of Calles
Mercaderes and Lamparilla -
✆ (7) 862 9293 - www.hotelconde
devillanueva.com - ▤ ✖ - 9 rooms,
162/240 CUC ⬚.* Ideally located on
Calle Mercaderes, the tourist heart
of Hababa Vieja, is this 18C palace
that will delight cigar lovers. The
the warm, spacious rooms bear the
names of famous brands of Havana.
Don't miss the cigar shop, Casa del
Habano, on the ground floor *(see
"Shopping" p. 66).*

13 Hotel Los Frailes – *Map II-C3* -
*Calle Brasil 8 (Teniente Rey) btwn
Oficios and Mercaderes - ✆ (7) 862
9383 -www.gaviotahotels.com/
en/hotels-in-cuba/old-havana/
hotel-los-frailes - ▤ ✖ - 22 rooms,
130/200 CUC ⬚.* In a particularly
well-located heritage building is
this hotel, which takes its name
("The Friars") from its vicinity to
San Francisco de Asís convent. The
monastic theme is applied throughout
the decor, including the staff uniform
of black robes. Comfortable and
peaceful.

22 Hostal Valencia – *Map II-C2* -
*Calle Oficios 53 at Obrapía -
✆ (7) 867 1037 - ▤ ✖ - 14 rooms,
150/170 CUC ⬚.* Just south of Plaza
de Armas is this beautiful colonial
house, typical of the 18C. Its large
rooms are well decorated. All
overlook a shaded patio, home to
restaurant La Paella, which is a bit
noisy at mealtimes.

23 Hotel Ambos Mundos –
Map III-A2 - *Calle Obispo 153 at
Mercaderes - ✆ (7) 860 9530 - ▤
✖ - 52 rooms, 150/240 CUC ⬚.* This
great hotel has become legendary
since Ernest Hemingway's extended
stay between 1932 and 1940. His
room on the penultimate floor has
been transformed into a museum.
Decorating the ground floor are
portraits of all the celebrities who
have stayed. The rooms preserve
the spirit of the 1930s (furniture,
woodwork, etc.). Take the elevator
to the roof terrace for a magnificent
view of the city and ocean.

24 Hotel Florida – *Map III-A2* -
*Corner of Calles Obispo and Cuba -
✆ (7) 862 4127 - ▤ ✖ - 25 rooms,
150/240 CUC ⬚.* In the heart of
Habana Vieja is this magnificently
restored former palace from 1835.
The refined rooms overlook a superb
neoclassical patio.

26 Hotel Santa Isabel – *Map III-B2* -
*Calle Baratillo 9 btwn Obispo and
N. López - ✆ (7) 860 8201 - ▤ ✖ -
27 rooms, 200/330 CUC ⬚ - Wifi.*
On the Plaza de Armas is one of the
most beautiful establishments in
Habana Vieja, with luxury, intimate

Hotel Ambos Mundos

atmosphere and the character of an 18C palace. The hotel has declined a bit in recent years, with a few maintenance issues throughout.

FROM THE CAPITAL TO THE PRADO

On the border of Habana Vieja and Centro Habana, the area around Parque Central was the heart of worldly life in the first half of the 20C. The area is home to some of the city's nicest hotels. These establishments don't have the colonial charm found in Habana Vieja but do meet international comfort standards.

Splurge

11 **Hotel Inglaterra** – *Map II-A3* - *Prado 416 btwn San Rafael and San Miguel* - ℰ *(7) 860 8596* - *www. hotelinglaterracuba.com* - 🖳 ✕

🅿 - *83 rooms, 111/292 CUC* 🍵 - *car rental, exchange office, medical services, wifi.* Right on Parque Central, next to the Gran Teatro, this 1875 building— a National Monument— combines Neoclassical architecture and historic charm, especially in its beautiful public areas. The rooms are comfortable and the location ideal as a base for wandering throughout the city.

14 **Hotel Sevilla** – *Map II-A2*- Calle *Trocadero 55 btwn Zulueta and Prado* - ℰ *(7) 860 8560* -*www. hotelsevilla-cuba.com* - 🖳 ✕ 🛋 🅿 - *178 rooms, 115/290 CUC* 🍵 - *car rental, exchange office, medical services, wifi.* Even if you're not staying here, this hotel, with its beautiful Moorish facade complete with decorative elements from the Royal Alcázar of Seville, is worth a visit. The bars and restaurants are open to the public. Its huge lobby is covered in *azulejos* (painted ceramic tiles). This hotel has an Andalusian spirit, drawing on Cuba's Spanish roots.

17 **Hotel Parque Central** – *Map II-A2* - *Calle Neptuno btwn Prado and Zulueta* - ✆ *(7) 860 6627* - *www. hotelparquecentral-cuba.com* - ▣ ✖ ⊡ - *427 rooms, 180/300 CUC* ⊡ - *rental cars, exchange and tourism offices, wifi.* Facing the square of the same name, this imposing modern building hosts many business travelers. Amenities include a bar and pool with panoramic views of the city.

21 **Hotel Saratoga** – *Map II-A3* - *Prado 603 at Dragones* - ✆ *(7) 866 1000* - *www.hotel-saratoga.com* - ▣ ✖ ⊡ - *96 rooms, from 300 CUC* ⊡ - *car rental, exchange and tourist offices, wifi.* Where can you swim in a rooftop pool within easy reach of the dome of the Capitol? The Saratoga, of course! This is the chicest address in Havana, priced accordingly. An institution since the end of the 19C.

21 **Hotel Telégrafo** – *Map II-A3* - *Prado 408 and Neptuno* - ✆ *(7) 861 1010* - ▣ ✖ - *63 rooms, 105/190 CUC* ⊡. Inaugurated in 1888 on Parque Central, this hotel remains a comfortable place to stay.

CENTRO HABANA

Mid-range

18 **Hostal Peregrino Consulado** – *Map II-A2* - *1/F, Consulado 152 btwn Colón and Trocadero* - ✆ *(7) 860 1257* - *www. hostalperegrino.com* - ▣ ✖ - *5 rooms, 45/65 CUC.* A large family apartment at the entrance to Centro Habana, not far from the Prado. The rooms are cozy; on the street side, they have little balconies. A pleasant welcome, with lots of good advice on how to discover Havana. The owners also have a casa in Habana Vieja (*Chacón 60 btwn Cuba and Aguiar*).

Splurge

32 **Hotel Terral** – *Map IV-C1* - *Corner of Malecón and Lealtad* - ✆ *(7) 860 2100* - *www.habaguanexhotels.com* - ▣ ✖ - *14 rooms, 135/240 CUC* ⊡. Right on the Malecón, this small contemporary hotel, opened in 2013, combines good design, clean lines, and shades of blue, reflecting a unison with the ocean on which it opens widely. A successful project, despite the traffic and a relatively remote location. The good here wifi is a treat!

VEDADO

☻ **Good to know** – Vedado is not walking distance from Habana Vieja, but its pretty tree-lined streets and Belle Epoque villas will take you back in time.

Budget

28 **Casa Iliana García** – *Map IV-A2* - *Calle 2 554 btwn 23 and 25* - ✆ *(7) 831 3329* - *2 rooms, 25 CUC.* Iliana is charming and all white, typical of the Vedado, a haven of freshness and cleanliness. Regretfully,

Hotel Sevilla

the noise from traffic on 23rd Street is easily heard, so pack earplugs. If you're not a light sleeper, this is a bright and spacious place where you feel good despite the noise.

Mid-range

㉗ Casa Betty y Armando Gutiérrez – *Map IV-B1* - *Ave. 21 62 btwn M and N* - ✆ *(7) 832 1876* - ▦ - *2 rooms, 46 CUC.* A large apartment at the top of a building next to La Rampa. You'll forget the hustle of the district in the casa's bright spaces, even if, unfortunately, the rooms do not escape the buzzing noise of the street. Simple comfort, but the location is very convenient and the hosts charming.

㉛ Hostal Silvia – *Map IV-A2* - *Paseo 602 btwn 25 and 27* - ✆ *(7) 833 4165* - *www.hostalsilvia.com* - ▦ - 🅿 - *4 rooms, 42 CUC.* In another city, this large 1925 residence would house an embassy; in Havana, it welcomes tourists passing through. Silvia offers the rare opportunity to sleep in a superb property at a budget rate. The house has been maintained like a treasure by the charming family that owns it. There's a large greenhouse, huge entrance hall, a beautiful lounge filled with art and antiques, and a roof terrace. The space is evocative of the splendor of Havana of yesteryear.

㉝ Casa Zoila Zayas Ulloa – *Map IV-A1* - *Apt. 1, Calle K 254 btwn 15 and 17* - ✆ *(7) 831 1764* - *alecarvajalgarcia@gmail.com* - ▦ - *2 rooms, 35 CUC.* Zoyla, an ebullient grandmother, welcomes you to her beautiful bourgeois house with a big smile. The house was built in 1925, and the living room, in particular, seems not to have changed since the revolution. Its old photos, barely faded, are remarkable.

Splurge

㉙ ⌂ Hotel Nacional – *IV-B1* - *Ave. 21 at Calle O* - ✆ *(7) 836 3564* - *www.hotelnacionaldecuba.com* - ▦ ✕ 🏊 🅿 - *457 rooms, 468/518 CUC ☕* - *car rental, exchange office, medical services, tennis, wifi.* Overlooking the Malecón, its Neoclassical architecture a landmark in Havana, is the city's most famous hotel. Inaugurated in 1930, it's a true historical monument. The sumptuous setting of its hall and lounges, the large swimming pool and the beautiful garden overlooking the ocean: everything creates a privileged, unspoilt setting. It is here that the Obama family stayed when they came to Cuba in March 2016.

㉚ Hotel Presidente – *Map IV-A1* - *Ave. 7ᵐᵃ (Calzada) 110 and Ave. de los Presidentes* - ✆ *(7) 838 1801* - *www.hotelrocpresidente.com* - ▦ ✕ 🏊 🅿 - *158 rooms, 130/200 CUC ☕* - *parking, tourist office, medical services, wifi.* This large hotel, opened in the 1920s, remains a luxurious enclave near the Malecón. Opulent lounges, comfortable rooms and quality service, for a mixed international clientele seeking an international standard.

Hotel Nacional

MIRAMAR

Farther from the city center than Vedado, Miramar requires a vehicle or generous taxi budget.

Mid-range

34 Casa Candy Mederos y Alejandro – *Map V-A2* - *Ave. 39 4408 btwn 44 and 46* - *℘ (7) 203 6958* - *alejandroalvm@yahoo.com* - 📧 **P** - *2 rooms, 35/40 CUC* 🛏. Imposing residence on the outskirts of Miramar. Inside, everything is spacious, and there's something majestic about the staircase leading to the bedrooms. The polished granite floor, with its black and white geometric patterns, impresses with its elegance and brilliance. Breakfast is served in the living room or in the garden, in the shade of mango and avocado trees.

35 Hotel Meliá Habana – *Map V-A1-2* - *Ave. 3ra btwn 76 and 80* - *℘ (7) 204 8500* - *www.melia.com* - 📧 🍴 🏊 **P** - *397 rooms, 170/280 CUC* 🛏 - *exchange office, medical services, fitness center, wifi.* This ultra-modern complex, overlooking the Atlantic Ocean, meets all the standards of a major international hotels: comfortable rooms, three pools, several restaurants, a fitness area and tennis courts, etc. Ideal for those looking for a holiday destination in Havana.

Short Trips from Havana

Varadero beach
© Nikada/iStockphoto.com

Varadero★★

Lying 140km/87mi east of Havana, this year-round destination for sunbathers and snorkelers covers the entire Hicacos Peninsula (see map p. 86), which is named for the shrubs that flourish here. Separated from the mainland by the Paso Malo lagoon, this narrow finger of land (20km/12mi long and a third of a mile wide) extends out between the Straits of Florida and Cárdenas Bay.

Long beaches of fine, silvery white sand stretch along the northern side all the way to Las Morlas. Loudspeakers at the resorts blast music all day; parties take place nightly in most of the hotels. Quieter beaches can be found close to the town side, at the western end of the peninsula.

The beaches and grand resort hotels are the main attractions, but visitors can also enjoy browsing through the markets of the town of Varadero itself, and seeing the handful of original ramshackle buildings.

Sun-washed streets are lined with sizable stone or wood villas (now small town hotels) that bear witness to the wealth of their former owners. The tip of the peninsula remains a semi-undeveloped wilderness, but hibiscus plants and other tropical vegetation are gradually being overtaken by yet more tourist-oriented vacation resorts.

82

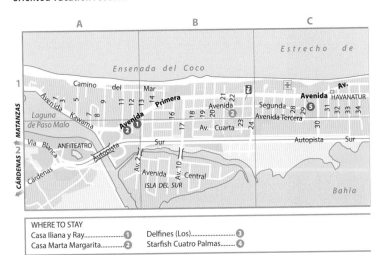

WHERE TO STAY	
Casa Iliana y Ray.....................❶	Delfines (Los).....................❸
Casa Marta Margarita.............❷	Starfish Cuatro Palmas.........❹

GETTING THERE FROM HAVANA

◆ **By Bus** – Omnibus Interprovincial Bus Station **(Map I, D2)**, corner of Calle 36 and Autopista Sur, ✆(45) 61 4886. Comfortable, air-conditioned **Víazul** buses run from Varadero to Havana four times a day: www. viazul.com or tourist offices.

◆ **By Taxi** – **Cubataxi** is the official company ✆(45) 61 4444.

GETTING AROUND

The Autopista Sur is the main artery along the peninsula. Getting around on foot is easy in town, but you'll need transportation to explore the rest of the peninsula.

◆ **By Bus** – The double-decker **Varadero Beach Tour** bus runs 9am-9pm throughout the downtown area along Ave. 1ra (every 15-30min) with 40+ stops. Tickets 5 CUC, valid all day for unlimited trips (*don't throw away your ticket!*).

◆ **By Taxi** – Cubataxi vehicles (with meters) park in front of most hotels. Fares outside the town of Varadero run about 40 CUC. Coco-taxis may be exorbitant. **Gran Car** classic car taxis are parked in the town end of Varadero (25 CUC/hr).

◆ **By Carriage** – Horsedrawn carriage rides downtown are 10 CUC per person per city tour.

83

WHERE TO EAT		
Casa del Chef (La)............... ❶	El Retiro................................ ❸	Terracita's Cafe........................... ❺
Castel Nuovo.......................... ❷	Paladar Nonna Tina.............. ❹	

- **Car Rental** – If you're staying in Varadero and not traveling beyond, renting a car is generally more expensive than taking a few short taxi rides. Expect to pay CUC 50 per day for a compact manual car. You can rent a car from **Havanautos** (*www.havanautos.com*), corner of Avenida 1 and Calle 8 **(Map I, A2)** or 31 **(Map I, C1)**, ℰ(45) 61 3733/4409. **Cubacar (Map I, B1)**, corner of Avenida 1 and Calle 31, ℰ(45) 66 7029. **Rex (Map 1, D2)**, Calle 36 across from the bus station, ℰ(45) 61 1818. *See also www.transturvaradero.com.*

- **Scooter Rentals** – Scooter rentals from Transtur **(Map I, B1)**, corner of Avenidia 1 and Calle 21 or corner of Calle 13 and Avenida 1; and at many hotels. 12 CUC/2 hours to 15 CUC/ half a day and 25 CUC/day.

VISITOR INFORMATION

- **Tourist information** – **Cubanacán** www.cubanacan.cu/en. **Infotur** has a desk in most large resorts. Head office in Hotel Acuazul at Avenida 1 and Calle 13.

- **Tourist Assistance** – Asistur - www.asistur.cu - corner of Calle 30 and Ave. 1ra. Ave. -ℰ(45) 66 7277 - (closed Sun) acts as the representative for foreign insurance companies in Cuba and offers aid to international travelers, including help with lost documents, hospital admission and repatriation. Legal and financial assistance also available.

24-hour emergency assistance: ℰ(7) 866 8339 or ℰ(7) 866 8527.

- **Accommodations/Dining** – *see Where to stay and Where to eat (p. 88).*

- **Banks/Currency exchange** – There are currency exchange desks are in most hotels. The following also exchange (as in Havana, USD, CAD, an Euros are best).

Banco Financiero Internacional (BFI), Avenida 1 and Calle 32 and Corner of Calle A and Avenida de Las Americas

Banco de Crédito y Comercio Avenida 1 between Calles 35 and 36.

Plaza América, KM 11 Autopista (there is also a BFI here).

- **Health** – Visitors in need of medical aid should go to the **Clínica Internacional**, corner of Avenida 1 and Calle 61; ℰ(45) 66 7711; there's also a 24-hour pharmacy.

Some **hotels** have medical services, and most can call a doctor to come to you.

WATERSPORTS AND OUTDOOR ACTIVITIES

- **Snorkeling and Diving**
ScubaLibre Varadero: ℰ(5) 263 4648; www.scubalibrevaradero.com

Varadiving: (5) 263 6525; www.varadiving.club

Las Antillas Diving Club: ℰ(5) 352 3555; ℰ+49 1575 2895 573 (Whatsapp); www.antillasdiving.com

Atlantis Varadero: ✆(5) 263 7732; www.scubaatlantisvaradero.com

Acuadive: ✆(5) 352 5949; www.acuadive.com

Playa Coral Diving: ✆(5) 289 0932;

◆ **Kiteboarding**

Caribbean Riders Kite School: ✆(5) 2772388; www.varadero kiteschool.com

◆ **Fishing and Boat Trips**

Marinas Gaviota: ✆(5) 569 8123; www.marinasgaviota.cu

◆ **Golf**

Varadero Golf Club, Mansión Xanadú (*see Hotels, Varadero*), ✆(45) 668 482; www.varaderogolfclub.com. 18-hole course; lessons available. Green fee US$100.

THE RESORT TOWN

Varadero is a full-size international enclave on Cuban soil. You'll certainly meet more Canadians and Europeans than Cubans due to the cost of staying at an all-inclusive hotel. It's a bit harsh but truthful to say that, overall, the atmosphere seems artificial because there is no real Cuban cultural experience. All bands are imported to entertain vacationers. Most Cubans who work at the hotels do not live in Varadero itself. The town of Varadero lies between the lake at the western end named Laguna Paso Malo and Calle 64. *Avenidas* (avenues, parallel to the beach) intersect with *calles* (streets, numbered from 1 to 64) in a standard grid-like pattern, which makes it easy for newcomers to find their way. Most stores and services catering to tourists are concentrated on the two main avenues, **Avenida Primera** and **Avenida Playa.**

Retiro Josone

Avenida 1 (Primera), btwn Calles 55 and 58. This former country retreat of a wealthy Basque native who managed the Arrechabala rum factory includes a 9ha/22acre park. The tropical oasis of palm trees is nice for biking or strolling, unless you prefer to row around its artificial lake. Four restaurants are located within the park (*Where to eat, p. 89*).

HICACOS PENINSULA

If you have a car, you can make this a driving tour of about two hours. If you don't, you can get the **Varadero Beach Tour bus** (*see p. 83*) or taxi to any of the places below. Luxury resorts have been spreading towards Punta Morlas, the easternmost part of Varadero. At the western entrance to Varadero, the Autopista Sur takes over from the Vía Blanca as the major highway continuing east.

◗ *Follow Avenida 1 east out of town onto the Autopista del Sur. After about 4km/2mi, take a left at the signpost.*

Mansión Xanadú

Built in 1930 for the French-born chemical magnate **Francis Irénée Du Pont de Nemours**, the mansion derives its better known name of **Xanadú** from Samuel Taylor Coleridge's poem hanging on one of its walls. Overlooking turquoise waters from the San Bernardino crags, the extravagant four-story mansion was once the centerpiece of a huge estate that included its own golf course, private beach, and gardens planted with coconut trees, flowers and vegetables. Turned into a boutique hotel *(Where to stay, p. 88)*, the former Du Pont family residence now offers guests a refined interior that measures up to the magnificent outdoor setting. Take in views of the coastline while sipping a cocktail in the top-floor bar to the backdrop of live jazz and Cuban traditional music, or dine in the Xanadú restaurant *(Where to eat, p. 89)*.

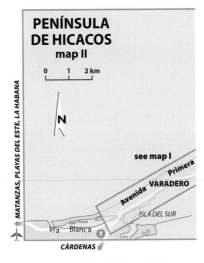

PENÍNSULA DE HICACOS
map II

0   1   2 km

N

MATANZAS, PLAYAS DEL ESTE, LA HABANA

see map I

Primera
VARADERO
Avenida

ISLA DEL SUR

Vía Blanca

CÁRDENAS

◖ *Get back on Autopista Sur, and drive north 5km/2.5mi. Then, continue north on Autopista Sur to a sign on the left of the highway pointing to Cueva Ambrosio.*

Parque Ecologico Varahicacos

Open daily 9am–4:30pm. 5 CUC for hiking trails, 5 CUC for cave (see listing below), 2 CUC for giant cactus Patriarca. This very pretty and well tended park is a nice break from the beach resorts. You can join **guided walks** along the park's trails or walk them on your own. They're well-marked and the paths are easy (though wear sneakers, not flip-flops). The park's three sites are Cueva Ambrosio; the **Cuevas Musulmanes,**

a 2,000-year-old burial site of 19C Cuban smugglers. These human remains are joined by lizards and birds who swoop in. Don't miss the 20-foot-tall, 500-year-old giant cactus called **El Patriarca.** It's believed to be the oldest living thing in the country.

Cueva Ambrosio

Open daily 9am–4:30pm. 5 CUC. This cave discovered in 1961 is decorated with red and black rock paintings from the pre-Hispanic period. Some of the drawings lend credence to the theory that runaway slaves may have found refuge here. What the cave is packed with, though, is bats. They're completely harmless, but not for the faint of heart. You can go in on your own (you'll be given a flashlight with your ticket) or follow the guide for an

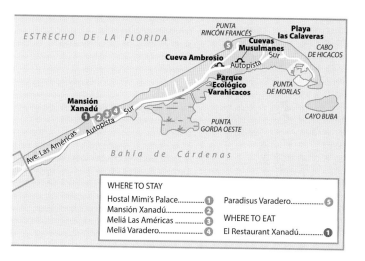

WHERE TO STAY

Hostal Mimi's Palace..............❶	Paradisus Varadero..................❺
Mansión Xanadú......................❷	
Meliá Las Américas ....❸	WHERE TO EAT
Meliá Varadero.......................❹	El Restaurant Xanadú.............❶

informative tour. The cave is located in the **Parque Ecológico Varahicacos,** a pristine coastal lagoon surrounded by woodland. This large protected area is known for its coastal birds (both local and migratory), and traces of ancient humans.

DAY TRIP FROM VARADERO TO MATANZAS★

42km/26mi west of Varadero.
Divided by the Yumurí and San Juan rivers, Matanzas (meaning "slaughter") was founded in 1693 on the site of an old slaughterhouse. Once a wealthy colonial town with a lively intellectual and cultural life, Matanzas today remains an active port, but there's not a lot going on here for visitors. Below are the attractions worth seeing (in the town center). On the outskirts of town are the fun Bellamar Caves.

◆ **By Bus:** There are four Viazul buses daily from Varadero to Matanzas *(6 CUC, see www.viazul.com).*
◆ **Taxi:** Shared taxis wait outside the bus station to gather passengers. This is a good option if you don't want to wait for the bus. For a private taxi from Varadero to Matanzas; expect to pay 50 CUC return.

Teatro Sauto★★
East side of the Plaza de la Vigía.
Visit by guided tour daily 9am–5pm; 2 CUC. This Neoclassical building (1863) was designed by Italian Daniele dell'Aglio, who painted the exquisite **ceiling**★★ in the main hall. French actress Sarah Bernhardt performed

Museo Farmacéutico

© Walter Bibikow/age fotostock

Cuevas de Bellamar (Bellamar Caves)★

3km/2mi southeast of Matanzas. Open daily 9:30am–5pm. 8 CUC (add 5 CUC to bring in a camera). Guided tours (1hr) available. Two restaurants on-site.

By Car/Taxi: From Plaza de la Vigía in Matanzas, cross the Calixto García bridge and proceed on Calle 272 for about a quarter of a mile. Turn right in front of the bus terminal. The caves are sign-posted to your left at the next intersection.

These caves were discovered in the mid-19C by a farm worker. The 3km/1.8mi of galleries open to the public are actually part of a much larger cave system. Pure crystal formations include **crystal lamps** of varying colors and natural limestone concretions bearing evocative names like Columbus' Cloak and Chapel of the Twelve Apostles. It's humid in here, can be crowded, and there are a lot of steps. The floor is slippery. Don't wear flip flops.

WHERE TO STAY

Most accommodations in Varadero are large, international resorts, many all-inclusive, offering multiple pools, swim-up bars, the works. You will not have difficulty finding a comfortable place with extensive facilities. We've listed below only *casas particulares* (guesthouses). Some are in the more authentic town of Santa Marta, near the airport, and 10 minutes' drive from the Varadero resort strip.

here in 1887 and Russian ballerina Anna Pavlova in 1915. The building underwent restoration in 2018.

Museo Farmacéutico★★★

Calle 83, south of Plaza de la Libertad, four blocks from Teatro Sauto. Open Mon–Sat 10am–5pm, Sun 9am–2pm. 3 CUC (add 1 CUC to take photos, which you will certainly want to do).
This pink building with a wrought-iron balcony houses an antique pharmacy founded in 1882 by a Frenchman who married into a respected Cuban family of pharmacists. Remarkably restored, the old store features porcelain jars imported from France, a bronze scale, and other curiosities. In the former **laboratory,** behind the inner courtyard, are a still, a cauldron and copper instruments.

3 **Hostal Mimi's Palace** – *Map II* - *Calle H 5, Santa Marta -* 📞 *(45) 619 034 -* 🍴 ✂ *- 4 rooms, 19 CUC* . The rooms here are modern and quite comfortable, on a quiet side street less than 10 minutes' walk from restaurants and bars and from the beach. Bikes available for rent. Tours can be organized.

Pedrito Hostal – *off map* - *3ra Oeste 106 btwn 12 and 13, Santa Marta -* 📞 *(5) 336 0551 -* 🍴 ✂ *- 4 rooms, 44 CUC.* Everyone staying at this casa is treated like family. Nothing is too much trouble: lending out free bicycles, organizing taxi services and tours, preparing heaping, delicious meals, and procuring good wine, no small feat in Cuba. This is a warm home with a lovely garden and four clean, comfortable, homey guestrooms.

1 **Casa Ileana y Ray** – *Map I-A2* -*Calle 41 108 btwn 1 and 2 -* 📞 *(45) 669 027, (5) 2920980 -* 🍴 ✂ *- 4 rooms, 50 CUC.* A block from the beach on a quiet side street is Illeana and Ray's guesthouse. Here, sun-baked travelers feel right at home in the two rooms and with resident dog Malu who hangs out on the patio. Walking distance to restaurants, bars, currency exchange, supermarket and a cigar shop.

2 **Casa Marta Margarita** – *Map I-A2* - *Avenida 2da 2101 at 21 -* 📞 *(45) 614304, (5) 8116 999 -* 🍴 ✂ *- 4 rooms, 50 CUC.* A block from the beach and walking distance to bars and restaurants is this comfortable

casa, which serves a tasty breakfast (no dinner). Pleasant garden with outdoor shower so you can rinse off after the beach even if you've checked out of your room.

WHERE TO EAT

5 **Terracita's Cafe** – *Map I-C1* - *2806 Ave 1ra btwn 28 and 29-* 📞 *(45) 612 514 - Daily except Sun 8am-10pm - 4 CUC.* The fare is simple but tasty at this inexpensive cafe a block in from the beach. For breakfast, coffee, eggs, fruit; for lunch and dinner sandwiches, burgers, Cuban-style pizza (don't expect anything you'd find in Italy), and grilled meats. A few vegetarian options.

2 **Xanadu** – *Map II* - *Inside Xanadu Mansion (Dupont House) hotel, Carretera Las Americas KM 8 1/2 Autopista Sur -* 📞 *(45) 668 482 - www.cubavaraderogolfclub.com/ en/club-house - Daily noon-11pm - 40 CUC.* The priciest restaurant in Varadero is inside a golf/club hotel on the beach. It's a popular spot for sunset cocktails at the third floor bar and for romantic dinners, with most diners opting for seafood.

4 **Paladar Nonna Tina** – *Map I-D1* - *5 Calle 38 btwn Aves. 1ra and Playa -* 📞 *(45) 612 450 - www.paladar-nonnatina.it - Daily except Mon. noon-11pm - 10 CUC.* When you need a break from Cuban fare, there's this Italian joint just off the beach, serving pasta, pizza, tiramisu, and cold beers. Friendly service, good for families.

89

Las Terrazas ★

▶ **75km/47mi southwest of Havana by the Autopista.**

▶ **Víazul buses** stop in Las Terrazas en route to Viñales. **Travel time** is approx. 1h15m (6 CUC). Your accommodations in Havana can arrange a taxi for you (expect CUC 80-90 return).

▶ **Entrance fee** 5 CUC. www.lasterrazas.cu.

Located in western Artemisa province, Las Terrazas (Spanish for "the terraces") is the best and most developed **ecotourism** project in Cuba. The tiny town is a wonderful day or overnight trip from Havana. This rural community (population 1,000) is part of the **Sierra del Rosario**, a designated UNESCO Biosphere Reserve encompassing a 26,686ha/103sq mi area of protected rivers, valleys and mountains that was cleared of natural forest by cattle ranches and coffee and tobacco plantations. In the late 1960s, when the degradation of the land left local farmers impoverished, a development plan for the Sierra region was launched. It involved **terracing** 5,000ha/19sq mi of hills that had been stripped of vegetation and reforesting them to stop erosion. It was successful; decades later, the Sierra's forests are regenerating.

The **Las Terrazas Tourism Complex** (1994), an eco-resort that is testament to the success of sustainable tourism, overlooks the village's attractive white houses cascading down to Lake San Juan.

ACTIVITIES

Zipline – Cruise through the forest on this fun 1.6km/1mi zipline for ages two and up. (*10 CUC for three sections, 20 CUC for all six. Discount for Hotel Moka guests.*)

Hiking – Marked **trails** in the Sierra del Rosario are dotted with waterfalls, natural pools and vestiges of old coffee plantations. Hotel Moka runs guided tours of varying length and difficulty (*www.lasterrazas.cu/en/excursion/list*). About 2km/1.2mi northeast of Las Terrazas, on Las Delicias hill, hikers can take a tour around the semi-restored **Cafetal Buenavista**, a coffee plantation built in 1801 by French refugees from Haiti. Coffee production at this site is no more, but a few pieces of antique coffee equipment remain, including a huge grindstone that took beans from their shells.

Museums and galleries – Overlooking the lake is Galería de Lester Campa (*daily, hours vary*) and, a few houses down, Casa-Museo Polo Montañez, the former home of lauded folk singer Polo Montañez (*Mon-Fri 9am-5pm*).

Las Terrazas, Sierra del Rosario Biosphere Reserve

Boating – Las Terrazas sits on small Lago del San Juan where you can swim or cruise around in row boats.

WHERE TO STAY

There are three types of accommodation at Las Terrazas: the very comfortable 42-room Hotel Moka, five guestrooms within locals' homes, and 11 rustic cabins with shared bathrooms and showers (they have electricity). *See www.lasterrazas. cu/en and be sure to book in advance.*

WHERE TO EAT

Cafe de Maria– *center of Las Terrazas - ℰ (48) 578 527 - Daily 8am-5pm - 2 CUC.* True, the only thing you'll be eating here is coffee, but we'd wager it'll be the best of your trip. On the menu are a dozen-plus coffees (cappuccino, cortado, americano). Have them hot, over ice, or with a splash of rum. The view from the open-air cafe is pretty as a postcard, with rolling green hills, thickets of tropical trees, and terracotta-tiled roofs.

El Romero– *center of Las Terrazas - ℰ (48) 578 555 - Daily noon-9pm - 10 CUC.* Vegetarians and anyone missing vegetables can rejoice at this homey restaurant where atop orange tablecloths sit baskets of housemade wholegrain bread and nicely plated savory crepes, salads with lovely little beets, and soups like potato cream and pumpkin. The menu changes a bit depending on what's available, as a good portion of the products used are grown at Las Terrazas.

Planning Your Trip

Playa Santa María del Mar, Playas del Este
© Walter Bibikow/hemis.fr

Know before you go

BUSINESS HOURS

Stores are usually open every day except Sunday from 10am to 6pm. In small towns shops sometimes close at lunchtime. Museums in this guide have their hours listed, though note that venues occassionally open later or close earlier than their posted hours.

BARGAINING

Bargaining is not a Cuban tradition but came with independent tourism. You can negotiate rates quoted by private taxi companies and classic car drivers.

CYCLING

It's surpringly hard to hire a bike in Havana. If your casa owner has one, or knows someone who does, they may rent it to you. Cycling around the quiet, shaded streets of Vedado and Miramar is nice. Cycling in Habana Vieja much less so; it's crowded and the pavement uneven.

CUSTOMS

If you have gifts in your luggage, their value should not exceed 50 CUC. You cannot carry more than 10kg of medications. Alcohol imports are limited to 3 liters, and you can bring no more than 200 cigarettes or 50 cigars. Questioning by customs officials is very rare. Importing firearms, explosive materials, and drugs is prohibited. The same is true for any fresh food items that have not been packaged (fruit, for example). Certain books or publications may be banned in Cuba, so choose your holiday reading accordingly.
You will without a doubt leave Cuba with rum and cigars in your luggage, but in limited quantities: 3 bottles of alcohol and 50 cigars. To fight against counterfeiting of cigars and the black market, customs officers may ask for proof of purchase (*comprobante*) when you're leaving the country. Animal and plant species are protected (turtles, coral etc.). If you are in posession of these species, they'll be confiscated and you'll pay a fine. Don't try to take them.

DRINKING WATER

Luxury hotels filter their tap water. If you're staying in a casa particular, your hosts will boil or purify water so it's safe for you to drink. To minimize plastic waste, buy large bottles of water as needed and fill a refillable water bottle. Filtering bottles like those made by LifeStraw are also an excellent, eco-friendly option.

ELECTRICITY

Though less frequent than before, **electricity outages** (*apagones*) still occur throughout the country. Hotels have their own generators, but for those who intend to stay in casas particulares, a small **flashlight** or headlamp will come in handy in the event of an outage. The power system is **110V/60 hertz**, with the same plugs used in the US, though some places also have 220V outlets.

EMBASSIES

Canadian Embassy– *Calle 30 518 at Ave. 7ma - ℰ (7) 204 2516 - www. canadainternational.gc.ca/cuba/index. aspx?lang=eng.*
US Embassy– *Calzada between L & M - ℰ (7) 839 4100- cu.usembassy.gov*
British Embassy– *Calle 34. 702 at Ave 7ma - ℰ (7) 214 2200-www. gov.uk/world/organisations/ british-embassy-havana*

ENTRY REQUIREMENTS

You should have a valid **passport** and the **Cuba Tourist Card** (*tarjeta del turista*), which must be handed over to Cuban authorities upon leaving the country. This is purchased from your airline upon check-in (*US$50, and some airlines charge their own fee*). If you book your trip through an agency, they will likely organize your Tourist Card.

The card is valid for no more than 30 days, but it can be renewed in Cuba for another 30 days maximum. In order to do that, you should obtain 25 CUC in stamps from an agency of Banco de Crédito y Comercio (Bandec), then take the stamps and your passport to la Dirección de Inmigracíon (in any big city). Opening hours: 8am-12pm, 1pm-3pm. To avoid long lines, it is best to go right when offices open.

🕭 **Good to know** – Whether you are a tourist or a business traveler, do not exceed the maximum length of stay of 30 days, even for one day, otherwise you risk being detained by immigration services.

In order to enter the country, visitors are required to **reserve one night at a hotel**. Customs officers will generally just ask for the name of the place and take your word for it. If you have the misfortune of being questioned by a meticulous officer and are unable to provide proof of reservation, you will have to reserve a room while at the airport.

GETTING TO HAVANA BY PLANE

Airport

José Martí International Airport –
📞 *(7) 266 4644 - www.isavia.is.*
18km/11mi sw from the city center.
A taxi from the airport is 25 CUC
depending on destination. Your casa
particular can organize airport pickup
for 25-30 CUC. There is no public
transport from the airport.

GIFT GIVING

Because of the shortages that affect
the country, everything you bring
in your luggage can double as a gift
as needed—clothing, perfume, pens
and pencils, lighters, toothbrushes,
soap, toothpaste, and food products.
Many of these have been inaccessible
for a large number of Cubans since
the beginning of 2011, when they
disappeared from the list of *libreta
(ration system)* products. This means
they can be bought in CUC, not in
CUP (*see Money p. 88*), a currency
unavailable to many Cubans. It's
likely that during your trip, someone
will go out of their way to help you.
It's nice to have small thank-you
gifts on hand. These can be playing
cards, a football, books in Spanish
or English. Basic **medications** (*see
Health p. 85*) are always welcome,
because they are sorely lacking and
very expensive. You may be invited
to someone's home, in which case a
bottle of rum, foreign cigarettes, or
something for kids is a welcome gift.
Though it may seem like a good idea,

don't just start handing out *plumas*
(pens) and *chicles* (gum) to groups of
kids who ask. It's much better to take
items to a school.

HABITS AND CUSTOMS

Meeting Cubans

This is easy if you speak Spanish
(and doable even if you don't). The
population is extremely warm and
spontaneous. Loner personalities
will feel bothered by incessant
solicitations, but anyone keen to
socialize will be rewarded with a
handful of new friends. Except for
Cubans who conduct small trade
with tourists, few interact regularly
with foreigners and will be pleased
to chat with you. For almost the
entire population, traveling abroad
represents an inaccessible dream. In
addition to administrative difficulties
with getting a permit to leave the
island, plane tickets are prohibitively
expensive. To them, you're relatively
interesting because you've come from
abroad.

Outside tourists zones, where
fewer visitors go, there are many
opportunities to meet Cubans. In a
country where asking for directions
can lead to a casual chat, every street
corner becomes the scene of multiple
conversations.

The most conventional way to mingle
with the population is to use the
private tourist circuit.
Sleeping in a guesthouse (*casa
particular*) and dining in *paladares*
(private restaurants) will give you a

glimpse into daily life in Havana. Your hosts will be happy to talk to you. If you stay in the same place for a few days, your circle of acquaintances is likely to spread to the rest of the family, as well as the neighbors. Do not be surprised to be invited to family and neighborhood fuctions. Prepare for this by packing extra things that can double as host gifts (see Gift Giving, p. 84).

Elegance

Cubans make it a point of honor to care for their appearance. While practical clothes are ideal for traveling around Cuba (though less necessary in Havana), pack one or two nice outfits. If locals invite you to go out, clean up and look sharp.

Dance

Dancing appears effortless for many Cubans, who sway expertly to the rhythm. Unless you are an extremely good dancer, this is probably not you. However, they'll be happy to teach you a few steps.

Politics

With foreigners, locals rarely speak of politics. Do not make them feel uncomfortable by addressing these topics. By the same token, they are happy to talk about the economic problems that the island is going through.

Standing in line

You will experience standing in line/queuing (hacer cola) at least once during your trip, if only to enjoy ice cream. Take a spot behind the last person in line while asking : "¿El último?" ("Last one?").

HEALTH

Heat

It's hot in Cuba, and humid. Using a good, strong sunscreen, wearing a hat, and a gradual exposure to the sun reduces the risk of sunburn and heat stroke. To avoid dehydration, it's important to drink a lot of water; always have a bottle with you (pack a reusable bottle). Don't be surprised if the humidity curbs your energy; even Cubans complain about it!

First-aid kit

You're not likely to need much in Havana, but because there are few well-stocked pharmacies, but it's smart to pack a small first-aid kit (band-aids, aspirin, antiseptic ointment, antihistamine, tablets for upset stomach). Be sure to pack sunscreen, bug spray, tampons (don't count on finding these), and a few packets of ear plugs. Before leaving Cuba, you can give your unused medicine to a hospital or clinic, or to your hosts if you're staying in a casa.

Illnesses

Thanks to an effective health policy, there aren't any tropical diseases in Cuba. The dengue fever virus struck the island, but a prevention campaign and the eradication of the Aedes mosquito drastically reduce the number of cases. Zika has not been a problem. Cases of chikungunya remain rare.

Mosquitos

During wet season, the risk of being bothered by mosquitoes is very real, although less so in big cities. Inside your room, turning on the aircon may keep them away, but the bravest ones will not be intimidated by so little. Spray yourself well with repellent. This is not such a problem in dry season. On some beaches, you will spot *jejenes*, flying insects resembling small mosquitoes but whose bites are 1,000 times more itchy. An antihistamine or anti-itch cream will bring some relief.

Medical services

For a long time, medicine was considered one of the successes of the Cuban Revolution, but the country suffers from a lack of equipment and medications. Clinics for foreigners are unaffected by the shortage and provide quality care. However, in the case of a serious problem, it's best to return to your country. Tourists should go to international clinics like **Servimed or** Clínica Central Cira Garcia Hospital. Doctors generally speak fluent English.

Stomach problems

A simple change in your diet can sometimes cause stomach problems, especially when the food is fattier than you're used to. You're unlikely to get food poisoning, but it never hurts to have some over the counter anti-diarrhea medicine and a few bags of herbal laxative tea in your suitcase.

HITCHHIKING

Due to a lack of public transportation, this is the most popular way for Cubans to move around. Hitchhiking (*coger botella)* is an organized venture. You'll see places with groups of people at the side of the road. An official called an *amarillo* (literally "yellow" because of the color of his uniform) stops state vehicles and divides people according to their destination. Hitchhiking in Cuba won't take you far on some routes. Keep in mind that for a Cuban, taking a foreign hitchhiker could result in a fine. If you're driving along the road, especially outside urban areas, you may feel guilty seeing mothers and their children waiting for an assumed vehicle under the blazing sun. Stop if you feel comfortable doing so (there is no penalty). It's a small kindness that goes a very long way.

HOLIDAYS AND CELEBRATIONS

January 1 – Liberation Day
May 1 – Labor Day
July 26 – National Rebellion Day
October 10 – Independence Day
There are other important dates that are widely celebrated but are not bank holidays. You will quickly discover that Cuba lives and breathes the lives of its independence patriots and revolutionaries: you won't miss those celebrations that usually take the form of a parade or inauguration of a statue. Here's the list:

January 28 – Birth of national hero José Martí

March 13 – Anniversary of the attack on Havana's presidential palace

April 19 – Bay of Pigs invasion victory

October 8 – Death of national hero Che Guevara

October 28 – Death of national hero Camilo Cienfuegos

December 7 – Death of national hero Antonio Maceo

INFORMATION

Call 113. In major hotels, you can consult the Directorio Turístico de Cuba, a **directory** listing all the numbers that are useful for foreigners. It is updated annually and is also available on the website **www.etecsa.cu** *(Spanish only)*.

INTERNET

Being thoroughly disconnected is one of the most exotic aspects of a trip to Cuba. Connections, where available, are very slow. As of this writing, Cubans who have mobile phones can access 3G service, and wifi is available in specified wifi parks (you can tell by the crowds of people on devices), and some hotels. You'll need a scratch card from state telecoms agency ETECSA (you can buy these at hotels, from people selling them in parks, and from ETECSA). Expect to pay 1.5-5 CUC for 1 hour depending on where you buy it. Despite increasing wifi hotspots, connections remain weak and slow. Try your luck in the morning, after people go to work. Note that sometimes your phone just will not connect to the network, and you'll quickly burn though the one-hour credit without ever getting online. Hotel networks are better than those in wifi parks.

MEDIA

Newspapers

The national daily (in Spanish) is **Granma**, the offical publication of the Communist Part of Cuba. There are weekly editions in foreign languages on sale in hotels. Large international resorts also stock some foreign newspapers and magazines, with a delay of several days.

Radio

Among Cuban radio stations, **Radio Taino** caters specifically to tourists, with some programs in English. It's possible to hear it even in Mexico and Florida. **Radio Reloj** is a 24-hour all-news live station founded in 1947. Information is presented in 60-second segments as the seconds tick by in the background. Some Cubans use it as an alarm clock, to leave on time for work or school; neighbors who stay at home go crazy listening to the throbbing countdown. If you rent a car equipped with a radio, you'll not escape it. Manu Chao used an excerpt from Radio Reloj in his song *Me Gustas Tú*.

99

TV

The two public TV channels are an integral part of daily Cuban life. Families would not miss for the world either an American movie on Saturday night or *telenovelas* (soap operas). **Cubavisión** and **Tele-Rebelde** start broadcasting at the end of the afternoon and stop around 11pm. Hotels also get some foreign channels via satellite.

MONEY

You need to get familiar with two currencies in circulation on the island—**peso cubano (CUP) and peso convertible (CUC)**—which, to add to the confusion, sometimes coexist under the same $ symbol. Currency in convertible pesos is marked INTUR (Institute of Tourism), while the national coins bear the words República de Cuba. At the time of publication of this guide, **1 CUC = approx. 26.5 pesos cubanos**.

Local currency

Cuban peso, the national currency *(moneda nacional)*, will not be of much use to you, except for small purchases at the market or from vendors; to pay for public transportation (bus, ferry); to make local calls from a phone booth; or to get the daily paper *Granma*. Traveling to Cuba without ever using the local currency is common.

Craft market

© Claire Boobbyer/Michelin

Foreigners are required to pay for tourist services (hotels, restaurants, plane tickets, car rental) in **convertible pesos (CUC)**. Cubans are increasingly using them to buy products that are absent from state stores. You will quickly learn to distinguish the shops, hotels and restaurants that use *moneda nacional* (CUP)—the ones that cannot accept foreigners, because they lack a license authorizing them to perform operations in foreign currencies— from those that are able to use *pesos convertibles (CUC)*. Therefore, almost all your payments will be made in *pesos convertibles (CUC)*. There are 100, 50, 20, 10, 5, 3 and 1 CUC bills and 1, 5, 10, 25, 50 and 100 cent coins (100 cents equal 1 peso). It's best to use small bills—maximum 20 CUC—so you have small change, since the currency is scarce outside tourist areas.

Currency exchange

Cuban banks, the network of *casas de cambio* Cadeca, and most major hotels exchange the main foreign currencies (EUR, USD, GBP, CAD). The convertible peso rate is generally pegged to the US dollar: **1 CUC =1 USD.** However, this can fluctuate if a low US dollar price penalizes the Cuban economy. A tax of 11-12% is added to any transaction made with a credit card. If your account is in another currency, such as euros, there is a second level of exchange. Expect some fluctuation in actual price when you evaluate your purchasing power. In order to avoid these extra costs,

it it's best to **arrive with a good amount of euros or dollars in cash**. You can then easily exchange these at a currency exchange window. (though queues can be long). Always keep some cash on you until your departure. Sometimes ATMs and credit card machines do not work, and you'll have no option but to pay in cash.

🙂 **Tip** –US credit and debit cards do not work in Cuba. Bring ample cash.

🙂 **Tip** – Don't forget to exchange your convertible pesos before leaving Cuba; they cannot be exchanged outside the country. You can do this at the airport.

🙂 **Tip** – At markets and some stalls, especially in places with few tourists, the price listed is in CUC, but the change will be given in CUP.

Banks

These are generally open Monday through Friday from 8am to 3pm (and later and until noon on weekends in big cities). Expect a line, but it will move fairly quickly.

Credit cards

Only **Visa International, Eurocard, Mastercard, Access** and **Banamex** cards are accepted. Note that As of this writing, **American Express is not accepted**. You can withdraw money at luxury hotels, branches of Banco Financiero Internacional or Banco Nacional de Cuba, and Cadeca offices. In theory, a number of tourist establishments accept credit cards. However, be prepared to use an alternative means of payment; payment machines are often broken and communication with authorization centers may be interrupted at any moment. There are no issues with credit card payments for car rentals and at luxury hotels. You can find ATMs in most towns, but they don't take all cards (mostly Visa; MasterCard holders routinely have to go to a bank to withdraw money).

MUSEUMS, MONUMENTS, AND SITES

Prices
Entrance fees vary from 1-3 CUC (up to 8 CUC for certain large Havana museums), with 1 CUC usually added for a guided visit. If you want to take pictures or video, you'll an extra 1-5 CUC). Entry into churches is free—unless they contain a museum—but donations are welcome.

Opening hours
In general, museums are open daily from 9am to 5pm, with frequent closures on Sunday afternoon and Monday. The hours listed in this guide were correct at publication, but note that opening hours are unreliable, and inadvertent closures common.

ORGANIZED TOURS

Cuba has a very extensive network of **state travel agencies**. The main ones are **Havanatur** (www.havanatur.cu), **Cubanacán** (www.cubanacan.cu) and **Cubatur** (www.cubatur.cu), and **Ecotur** (www.ecoturcuba.tur.cu), more oriented towards hikes and nature outings. These agencies offer various tour packages in and around Havana and the rest of the country. For travelers who want to be semi independent, you take day trips to the coast or a tobacco plantation). Most of these agencies, which are associated with large, state-owned hotels, also offer all-inclusive holiday packages at competitive prices.

PHONE

International calls
On a landline, you'll only be able to call abroad by using phone cards worth 5, 10 or 20 CUC, which can be bought in Telepuntos, small kiosks or outpost of state telecom agency **ETECSA**. There are **blue phonebooths** in all tourist places. Get a phone card with a code, rather than the chip, as the chip readers rarely work. Calls abroad are quite expensive. Depending on your mobile phone provider's roaming charges, it can make more sense to use that. Or, if you have a solid internet connection, use a VOIP service like Skype.

Local calls
If you're staying in a casa particular, they may or may not have a landline. They will have a mobile and will let you use it (possibly for a small fee). On the street are old public phones that work with 1 peso coins (national currency). These tend to work only within the city, so you can call places in Havana but nowhere else.

MOBILE PHONES

The cellular network works relatively well in Cuba, but the local cost of calls from landlines to Cuban mobiles is very high. Keep in mind that when you call on a mobile, the person you're calling also pays for the call. Mobile numbers usually start with 53 and consist of 7 digits.

PHOTOGRAPHY

Cubans love to be photographed and willingly pose if you ask them, especially if you write down their address to send them their portrait. Better yet, bring a Polaroid camera, which will bring people great joy. In museums and when visiting certain monuments, you often have to pay to take photos (sometimes up to 5 CUC!).

POSTAL SERVICES

Mail

Even though this once-common phenomenon has dwindled with the Internet, it may happen that some Cubans will entrust you with letters for their friends residing abroad, for you mail once back in your home country. This is the fastest and most reliable way, given that mail takes **between 3 weeks and 2 months** to cross the Atlantic. The typical route is for those who are not in a hurry. Stamps *(sellos)* are available at post offices, in hotels (0.6 CUC for a postcard) and in some shops selling postcards. Watch out for stamps in Cuban pesos, valid only for domestic mail. For urgent shipments or parcels, use **DHL** (www.dhl.com).

Post offices

Post offices are generally open daily, except Sunday, from 8am to 6pm. Major hotels can mail postcards for you.

SAFETY

Havana is generally quite safe. As with anywhere, avoid unlit and empty streets at night. Especially when walking in Habana Vieja, watch out for potholes and uneven cobblestones and sidewalks.

SEASONS

When to go depends on the type of trip you want to have: summer is better for a seaside stay, whereas winter is nicer for cultural visits. In **February**, **March** and **April** you can do both, while avoiding the high tourist season (December-January and July-August). Hurricane season in June through November, though it's September and October that have the highest chances of hurricanes.

SOLO TRAVEL

You will rarely be alone. Cubans are very open and will not fail to approach you to chat, help you find your way, or invite you to share their meal, which can lead to endless opportunities for encounters, especially if you have basic Spanish skills.

Women can safely travel alone. That's not to say that men won't make verbal advances. To politely repel them, turn a deaf ear to their pick-up lines or feel free to make it clear that you're not interested. If you feel uncomfortable, try to walk near groups of women or with families.

Men traveling alone likewise may face attempted pickups from sex workers; politely turn them down and walk away.

Do be aware of a **luchador**, a person who will try to rip off the tourist by various means. This word now tends to replace **jinetero**, a term used more and more for someone soliciting sex. A typical scam takes place upon entering a city, where a luchador will tell you your *casa particular* is closed, in order to take you to another one that will pay them a commission (the price of your room will therefore be higher).

Another tactic: you are looking for your guesthouse, La Casa de Maria, and you are taken to the home of "aunt Maria", of course with whom they are obviously not related.

Paladares recommended to you on the street will inevitably be described as the best of the district, but they generally are not, and you will overpay. It's better to get directions from policemen, taxi drivers (usually both Spanish only), shopkeepers, or your casa owners.

Coco-taxi

© akturer/Shutterstock.com

STREET ADDRESSES

Addresses in this book are listed as street name first, followed by the number, then one or two cross streets. Convento de Santa Clara, Cuba 610 btwn Sol and Luz means that the convent is located on Cuba Street, number 610, between Sol and Luz streets. If the building sits at the corner, usually only the two perpendicular streets are mentioned: Ambos Hotel Mundos, on Obispo and Mercaderes means it's at the corner of Obispo and Mercaderes streets.

☞ **Good to know** – In big cities, most streets names were changed after the revolution, but their old names are still very often used by Cubans: that's why maps may show the current street names while Cubans use others.

TAXIS

The **official taxis of Cubataxi** park in front of airports and most hotels. You will recognize them by the sign on the roof. Cars are usually comfortable and air-conditioned. All have meters; if your driver says theirs is broken, find another car. Drivers may offer the ride without using the meter, to avoid having to pay taxes; this can sometimes work to your advantage, as the ride will cost less. Confirm with your hotel or casa before you go out how much your ride should cost. The price of the ride varies based on the car. Traveling in a tiny Lada ends up a little cheaper than in a Peugeot, Hyundai or Volkswagen. When you

sit down, you'll understand why. Still, a trip in a Lada, even with squished kneecaps, can create great memories. For long rides or one-day tours, it's cheaper to rent a car or hire a driver than to use a yellow taxi.

Private taxis (maquinas)—often old American cars from the 1950s or Ladas, repaired and repainted multiple times—are licensed and cost less than yellow cabs These don't have meters, so agree on a price before you set off.

Communal taxis (colectivos) are big old American cars that follow fixed routes, generally major streets such as Calle 23 or Malecón, and stop on request. During peak times, five or six people pile up inside and there is rarely an empty inch left. The price of the ride is a modest 10 Cuban pesos. People will offer to transport you in their own vehicle. The service offered by these **personal cars** (carros particulares) is cheaper than other taxis. Reliability varies, but if your casa puts you in touch, you're good to go. In general, drivers will approach you to offer their services, for a few hours or several days. Negotiate the fare in advance and clarify who pays for gas.

Coco-taxis (a type of moto-rickshaw) and **bike-taxis** and are ideal for short rides around Havana. Set the price before the ride begins.

How to say it in Spanish

NUMBERS

One — Uno
Two — Dos
Three — Tres
Four— Cuatro
Five— Cinco
Six— Seis
Seven— Siete
Eight— Ocho
Nine— Nueve
Ten— Diez

GREETINGS

Hello — Hola
How are you? — Cómo estás?
Well, thank you — Bien, gracias
Please — Por favor
Thank you — Gracias
Pardon/excuse me — Perdóname/
disculpe
What's your name? — Cómo te
llamas?
My name is...— Me llamo/llama...
Nice to meet you — Mucho gusto
Goodbye — Adiós
See you later — Hasta luego

ASKING FOR THINGS

I want...— Quiero...
We want...— Queremos...
How much does it cost? — Cuanto
cuesta?...
A taxi, please — Un taxi, por favor
I don't understand — No entiendo
Do you speak English?— Hablas
Inglés?

DIRECTIONS

Left — Izquierda
Right — Derecha
Here — Aqui/Aca
There — Alli
At the corner — En la esquina
A una cuadra — In one block
Upstairs — Arriba
Downstairs — Abajo
Inside — Dentro
Outside — Afuera
The beach — La playa
The museum — El museo
The restaurant — El restaurante
The pharmacy — El farmacia

GETTING AROUND

Where is...? —Dónde está...?
The bathroom — El baño
The bank — El banco
The bus station — La estación de bus
[Street name] — La calle de...
I'm going to...— Voy a...
Please wait for me — por favor,
espérame
How much is a ticket to...— Cuánto
cuesta un boleto para ...
One ticket to...please — Un boleto
para ...por favor
I'm lost — Estoy perdido

QUESTIONS

I have a question — Tengo una
pregunta
Who — Quién
What — Qué

Where — Dónde
When — Cuándo
Why — Por qué
How — Cómo
What time is it? — que hora es?

EATING

A bottle of beer/water, please — Una botella de cerveza/agua, por favor.
A menu, please —Un menú, por favor
Rice — arroz
Chicken — pollo
Pork — cerdo
Beef — varne de vaca/res
Rice and beans — arroz congri or moros y cristianos
Ropa vieja — shredded/stewed beef in sauce
Lechon asado — grilled or roasted pig with crispy skin
Loho ahumado — smoked pork (cooked)
Ajiaco — Stew with corn, plantains, squash, and meat
Medianoche— sandwich on egg bread of ham, pork, cheese and pickles, so called because it's served at clubs after midnight
Pulpeta— meatloaf
Fish — pescado
Shrimp/prawns — camarónes/langostinos
Garlic — ajo
Sweet plantains — maduros
Ice cream — helado
Popsicle — paleta

I'm a vegetarian — Soy vegetariano
I have an allergy to...— Tengo una alergia a ...
Nuts/shellfish/gluten — nueces/mariscos/gluten

AT THE BEACH

An umbrella — un paraguas or una sombrilla
A towel — Una toalla
A chair — Una silla
A coconut (two, three...) — Un coco (dos cocos, tres cocos...)
Rum — ron

AT THE PHARMACY

(All pharmacists in Havana speak some English)

I have a headache —Tengo dolor de cabeza
...a stomachache — dolor de estómago
...mosquito bites — picaduras de mosquitos
...diarrhea — diarrea
I can't poop — No puedo hacer caca
Do you have band-aids? — Tienes curitas?

Find Out More

School children in Havana
© APproductions/iStockphoto.com

Festivals and events

Listed below is a selection of Havana's most popular annual events (dates and times may vary; check in advance). For details contact Infotur, the National Office of Tourist Information run by the Cuban Ministry of Tourism: (7) 204 0624, (7) 204 6635 or www.infotur.cu, or the Ministry of Culture: www.min.cult.cu (in Spanish).

JANUARY/FEBRUARY

Liberation Day– Every **January 1,** celebrants come to Havana's Plaza de la Revolución to commemorate the historic day of liberation as a result of Fidel Castro's 1959 revolution. The day is a public holiday for all Cubans.
Chinese New Year – Chinatown's grandest celebration is held the **during Chinese New Year** (based on lunar calendar so late Jan to mid Feb), when the lunar New Year is welcomed in by residents of Havana's Barrio Chino. Festivities include a dragon parade, fireworks, lion dances and family reunions. The Cuban School of Wushu also presents a display of martial arts.
Feria Internacional del Libro de La Habana – Sponsored in **February** by local bookstores and literary organizations, Havana's Book Festival means public readings, special presentations and browsing through lots of titles, as well the announcement of the prestigious Latin American writers' awards. The main venue is usually Fort San Carlos de la Cabaña. *www.cubaliteraria.com*
Festival del Habano – This popular event scheduled near the **end of**

February sees the gathering of cigar lovers from all over the world for tastings, cigar-rolling lessons, factory tours, a gala dinner and other events. *www.festivaldelhabano.com.*

MARCH/APRIL

Varadero Gourmet International Festival – The Ministry of Tourism of Cuba and the Palmares S.A. invite the public to this food festival held each **April** at the Plaza América Convention Hall in Varadero.

MAY/JUNE

Primero de Mayo – A tribute to the workers of the world, the **1st of May** celebration is devoted to parades, political speeches and flag waving in Havana's Plaza de la Revolución, an event that draws huge crowds.
Festival Internacional de Poesía de La Habana – Sponsored by Cuba's Writers' and Artists' Union (La Unión de Escritores y Artistas de Cuba), this **May event** attracts poets from around the world for readings and workshops as part of an international cultural exchange. *www.cubapoesia.cult.cu/en*

Religious Festivals

Las Charangas de Bejucal (*principally held December 24*) *are a mix of carnival, dance and sideshows held in the town of Bejucal, some 15km/9mi south of central Havana. Floats—up to 20m/65ft high and covered in lights—are created by two competing groups, La Ceiba de Plata and La Espina de Oro which, over the course of the night, try to outdo each others' floats with more decoration and dancers garlanding the towering carnival structures.*

The origin of the rival groups dates back to the times when Roman Catholics and their black slaves took to the streets to honor their deities; today, membership into either group is based on family history or individual preference. **Nochebuena** (*December 24*) *is celebrated in churches throughout Havana and at home, with Cubans roasting a pig in celebration. Each December 17* **St. Lazarus' Day** *is celebrated at the sanctuary of El Rincón, near Santiago de Las Vegas. Thousands of pilgrims come from Havana, some crawling all the way on their knees, to honor the patron saint of lepers and the poor.* **Nuestra Señora de la Caridad** *is the patron saint of Cuba. Her feast day (September 8) is celebrated with a procession in Centro Habana on the Sunday before this date, and at churches named in her honor. The most impressive one is held by the parish of Nuestra Señora de la Caridad del Cobre on Calle Salud. The feast of* **Nuestra Señora de la Candelaria** (*February 2*) *is celebrated at the Ermita de la Candelaria in Guanabacoa with a procession. The* **Feast of San Juan Bautista** *is celebrated between June 21 and 25 in San Miguel del Padrón; on June 24 an image of Saint John the Baptist is burned. The feast day is celebrated with music, food stalls and children's activities in this Havana municipality, located southeast of central Havana.*

Feria Internacional CUBADISCO – One of the country's biggest musical events, Feria Internacional CUBADISCO draws foreign production companies as well as Cuban music producers **every May** to this combination trade fair and festival. Concerts are staged primarily at Pabellón Cuba in Vedado but occur throughout the city, and musical awards are handed out.

Hemingway International Billfish Tournament – Marina Hemingway fills fishing fans at this annual tournament held in **June**.

Coloquio Internacional Ernest Hemingway – Usually held **every two years** in **late June** at the Hotel Ambos Mundos and Museo Hemingway, this symposium on the famed American writer is organized by the Consejo Nacional de Patrimonio Cultural. Many aspects of Hemingway's life and writings are presented and discussed, such as his fascination with bullfighting and his knowledge of Cuba.

JULY/AUGUST

Carnaval de La Habana – The pinnacle of Havana's annual celebrations, on **weekends in August**, Carnaval means evening parades with celebrants in creative costumes dancing to live music along the Malécon and in front of the Capitolio. Giant caricatures of popular figures called Muñecones and Gigantes are a highlight of the parades.

26 July (Revolution Day) – This important date in Cuba's revolutionary history, a public holiday, is honored with political speeches on TV and patriotic banners in the streets. It marks the birthday of Cuban patriot José Martí, as well as Fidel Castro's failed assault on the Moncada barracks in Santiago de Cuba in 1953.

SEPTEMBER/OCTOBER

Festival Internacional de Ballet – A highlight for ballet lovers around the world, this major biennial event, held in **late October** through **early November**, presents gala performances of both classical and modern ballet by various dance companies as well as the Cuban National Ballet at the Gran Teatro de La Habana, Teatro Mella, and Teatro Nacional. *www.festivalballethabana. cult.cu* (in Spanish).

Festival de Teatro de La Habana – Held in **October/November**, this 10-day theater festival is celebrated with performances for adults and children, as well as workshops in Havana's theaters. Cuban and international theater groups stage productions of Cuban classics as well as contemporary works. *www.fth. cult.cu*

Ernest Hemingway International Blue Marlin Fishing Tournament – Sport-fishing aficionados descend on Marina Hemingway in **September** for this annual event that was started by the writer himself.

NOVEMBER/DECEMBER

Havana Biennial – Occurring **every three years** (despite the name that alludes to two years), this prestigious event brings contemporary art shows to the Museo Nacional de Bellas Artes and other locations in Habana Vieja. The month-long cultural show is devoted to the art of Latin America and the developing world and features all media. The next Biennial will be held in 2018. *www. bienalhabana.cult.cu*

Nuestra Señora de las Mercedes – On **November 16**, Old Havana celebrates Our Lady of the Mercedes, while the founding of the city is commemorated with an ancient ritual in El Templete garden. In front of El Templete is a ceiba tree *(see p. 29)* that symbolizes the founding of the city. Citizens circle the tree three times, offer money, and embrace and kiss the tree.

International New Latin American Film Festival – Held in **early to mid-December**, this 10-day film festival showcases the latest Cuban, Latin American and even American productions. Screenings and seminars

International New Latin American Film Festival

take place in dozens of cinemas in Havana, but mostly in Vedado, and are often followed by parties. The festival is headquartered at the Hotel Nacional in Vedado. *www. habanafilmfestival.com.*

Marabana Marathon – Held the **3rd Sunday of November each year**, this sporting event attracts thousands of runners from many countries to participate in a marathon, half marathon, or 10K; the courses wind through Habana Vieja, Centro Habana and Vedado. This is Cuba's largest running event and hugely popular. *www.mapoma.es/marabana/en*

Salón Internacional de Arte Digital – Held in **November** in various city venues, this week-long event brings practitioners of the digital arts to Havana for demonstrations, talks and exhibits of the latest in the print and audio-visual media.

Havana Jazz Festival – Held four days in **mid-December**, this renowned festival features local and international talent performing in such venues as the Casa de la Cultura Plaza and Teatro Nacional de Cuba.

A timeless city

*Havana holds its visitors spellbound for many reasons, but it's the city's mixture of **architectural styles**—from Spanish Colonial and Moorish to Neoclassical and Art Deco—that makes the place seem so timeless. Splendid façades evoke a glamorous but faded past, especially along the waterfront—the magnificent **Malecón**—where sun, seaspray and tropical downpours have dimmed, but not erased, a palette of pastel colors. Many of the buildings here are being restored, thanks to an influx of foreign investment. Behind the seafront lies the city's colonial core, a labyrinth of alleyways, cracked sidewalks and dilapidated but still grand buildings, overhung by headily scented flowers. To the west, a few skyscrapers and once-fine villas mark wide avenues where luxuriant tropical vegetation seems to smother everything with its exuberant growth.*

Every year on November 16, in the gardens of El Templete, the people of Havana commemorate the anniversary of the **founding** of their city. On this day, in 1519, Spanish conquistadors held a solemn Mass to mark the founding of the town of **San Cristóbal de la Habana,** which had been moved twice from its original site. The town is said to have been named for **Habaguanex**, a native chief, although some historians believe the name derives from the word "haven", in reference to the harbor to whose development the city's fortunes have been closely tied. The town's strategic position between the Americas and Spain proved a boon to economic growth. Tradesmen set up shop around the harbor to gain access to ships loaded with sugar, gold, silver, tobacco, slaves and precious minerals. In the wake of

these wealth-laden ships, however, came pirates and buccaneers in the pay of Spain's European rivals. Between 1538 and 1544 the **Castillo de la Real Fuerza** was constructed to protect the city from incessant pillaging.

Despite such measures, Havana was seized in 1555 by Jacques de Sores, a French privateer. New fortifications were quickly built, and commerce flourished more than ever. In the mid-16C, Cuba's rulers moved the seat of government from Santiago de Cuba to more prosperous Havana, which became the official **capital of Cuba** in 1607.

Havana was attacked repeatedly by the British throughout the 17C and 18C. On August 13, 1762, the city fell into the hands of the English after two continuous months of siege. Less than a year later, under the terms of the

Havana's Diverse Population

Ever since Cuba was first colonized, successive waves of immigration have resulted in a mingling of different races with the **indigenous peoples** who were on the island at the time of Columbus' landfall. Most of the Europeans who colonized Cuba were **Spaniards.** There were sharp distinctions between people from Spain and those of Spanish origin born in Cuba, referred to as criollos (creoles). At the end of the 18C, **French** immigrants arrived, fleeing the slave revolt on Haiti. A century later, incoming fortune-seekers from Europe included people from France, Germany, Italy and Great Britain. Cuba's past link with what was then the Soviet Union meant an influx of **Russians,** a number of whom have remained here. From the 16C to the abolition of slavery in 1886, **West Africans** were shipped to Cuba as slave labor. Intermarriage between slaves and Hispanics saw the rise of the mestizo population. A person of mixed race in Cuba is known as a mulatto—a large portion of the population. The tiny **Chinese** presence in Cuba is visible in Havana's barrio chino (Chinatown); ships bringing Cantonese workers first landed in Cuba in 1847. Today, however, the Chinese comprise only about .1 percent of the population.

115

Barrio Chino

The Island's Main Religions

Cuba is a secular country in which freedom of worship is guaranteed, though after the Revolution, an attempt was made to marginalize religion in national life. In 1991, however, the 4th Communist Party Congress decided that Party members should again be free to practice the religion of their choice. In 1996 Fidel Castro was received at the Vatican by Pope John-Paul II, and in 1998 the Pope's visit to Cuba was a major event that also saw Cuba reinstate Christmas as a public holiday. The third papal visit was in 2015; Pope Francis, the first Latin American pope, was received with great enthusiasm by crowds in Havana, Holguín, and Santiago.

*Spanish colonial rule ensured that **Roman Catholicism** became the country's dominant religion. Cuba also has around 500,000 **Protestants,** the result of North American influence in the early part of the 20C. There is also a small **Jewish** community that maintains three synagogues in Havana. One small mosque, Havana's only one, serves Cuba's **Muslim** population, which is reported to be growing.*

Santería, *the religion practiced by the Yoruba people of southeastern Nigeria, has many followers in Cuba. An example of increased official tolerance of Santería was Fidel Castro's formal welcoming of the ruler of the Yoruba to Cuba in 1987. Covering a range of Afro-Cuban beliefs, Santería emerged here when imported African slaves fused the worship of African deities with Roman Catholicism. About 20 of the 400 Yoruba **orishas** (gods) are worshipped in Cuba.*

Treaty of Fontainebleau, Cuba was transferred back to Spain in exchange for Florida.

At the end of the 18C, the whole of the American continent was gripped by the desire for independence. By 1825 only Puerto Rico and Cuba remained under Spanish rule. Slavery continued to be a mainstay of colonial society; final emancipation came in 1886, following the end of the first (1868-1878) of two **wars of independence**. The explosion aboard the **USS Maine** in Havana harbor in February 1898 prompted the US to send troops to Cuba. Spain was soon defeated, and formally gave up its colony at the signing of the **Treaty of Paris** on December 10, 1898, at which no Cuban delegation was present. More than a half a century later, the **Cuban Revolution** (1953-59), led by Fidel Castro and Che Guevara, is seen by some as belated revenge for this snub to a proud country.

In the 19C Havana grew beyond the historic boundaries of its fortifications which, except for the defenses at the harbor entrance, were largely demolished in 1863. Development bypassed the city's historic heart, which became known as **La Habana Vieja** (Old Havana), and centered instead on newer districts to the west,

Ministry of the Interior building, Plaza de la Revolución

© YangYin/iStockphoto.com

117

such as **Centro Habana.** After Cuba became a republic in 1902, **Vedado** and **Miramar** saw major development. Letters and numbers were used to designate streets in these districts, which were laid out on a grid similar to American urban plans. American investors erected luxury hotels, gambling casinos and magnificent villas along the Almendares River. Following the **Revolution,** the city was purged of its casinos and brothels, and many of the elegant mansions were requisitioned away from private ownership.

Recent years have seen modern hotels being upgraded to cater to international visitors, and additional grand colonial buildings in Old Havana—a **UNESCO World Heritage Site**—being painstakingly restored. More and more *habaneros* are opening their homes as charming lodgings and as family-run restaurants to serve a steadily growing tourism trade.

Index

Photo credits

Page 4
Plaza Vieja: © golero/iStockphoto.com
Farmacia y Droguería Taquechel: © Claire Boobbyer/Michelin
Cementerio de Cristóbal Colón: © imantsu/iStockphoto.com
Plaza de la Catedral: © taikrixel/iStockphoto.com
Vintage car tour: © Bim/iStockphoto.com

Page 5
The Malecón: © redtea/iStockphoto.com
Palacio de los Capitanes Generales: © Claire Boobbyer/Michelin
Casa de la Obrapía: © Franck Guiziou/hemis.fr
Calle Mercaderes: © Matyas Rehak/Shutterstock
Gran Teatro de La Habana: © Photoservice/iStockphoto.com

Maps

Inside
La Habana Vieja *p16*
La Habana Vieja; Historic Center
    p22
La Habana;
    Vedado-Centro Habana *p40-41*
Cementerio de Cristóbal Colón
    p49
La Habana;
    Miramar and Playa *p51*
Varadero
    p82-83
Península de Hicacos
    p86-87

Cover
La Habana
    inside front cover

Detachable map
Havana *inside cover*

124

THE GREEN GUIDE short-stays **Havana**

Editorial Director	Cynthia Ochterbeck
Editor	Sophie Friedman
Contributing Writers	**Julie Schwietert Collazo, Sophie Friedman**
Production Manager	Natasha George
Cartography	Peter Wrenn, Theodor Cepraga
Picture Editor	Yoshimi Kanazawa
Interior Design	Laurent Muller
Layout	Natasha George

Contact Us	Michelin Travel and Lifestyle North America One Parkway South Greenville, SC 29615 USA travel.lifestyle@us.michelin.com
	Michelin Travel Partner Hannay House 39 Clarendon Road Watford, Herts WD17 1JA UK ☎01923 205240 travelpubsales@uk.michelin.com www.viamichelin.co.uk
Special Sales	For information regarding bulk sales, customized editions and premium sales, please contact us at: travel.lifestyle@us.michelin.com

**YOUR OPINION IS ESSENTIAL
TO IMPROVING OUR PRODUCTS**

Help us by answering the
questionnaire on our website:
satisfaction.michelin.com

Michelin Travel Partner

Société par actions simplifiées au capital de 15 044 940 EUR
27 cours de l'Ile Seguin - 92100 Boulogne Billancourt (France)
R.C.S. Nanterre 433 677 721

ISBN 978-2-067239-93-7
Printed: June 2019
Printer: ESTIMPRIM